# Table of Conten

# Acknowledgements

## Photography: Ryall Stewart
## Graphics Design: Ryall Stewart
## Editing: Jo Salata

# Preface

This book will show my unique way of teaching that has provided instant gratification on the tennis court for every student. It's a technique that has proven results on the spot. This book will give you a unique insight on strokes, technique, and basic strategy that is broken down in simple instruction that you might not have read in any other instructional books or seen on any videos. Over and over again so many of my students have been impressed with my teaching techniques that have improved their tennis instantly. You'll find that this book is quite different than any other book or video you might have seen or read. Countless times students have said to me, "This is fantastic I've never heard this before, and I can't believe how incredibly well it works because it makes so much sense. I just don't understand why haven't I heard it before. It's too bad I didn't have you as my instructor when I first started playing tennis." Regardless of whenever one chooses to start playing the game, or the age or level of the student, my technique in teaching starts by building the best possible foundation so the rest of your game improves rapidly. Once you develop the best foundation possible, it's what I like to refer to as the "mother of all foundations" in tennis, it's only then that you'll start feeling a tremendous amount of confidence in your strokes. This book breaks it down in such easy terms that someone who has never picked up a racket before will be able to relate and understand it, and my technique of teaching easily promotes interest in the game for all students. So be prepared to learn a lot, to be patient, and most importantly, to have fun.

Like anything else, learning the tricks of the trade can make doing whatever it may be much easier. It is the same with tennis. The game of tennis requires you to use all your muscles and forces you to think. By learning the tricks of the trade in tennis it will make playing the game a lot more fun as long as you understand proper technique and the subtle tricks that make playing this game easier. In tennis small adjustments will make a monumental difference when you learn how to do it the correct way. You'll also learn the unique art of how to accurately place your shots without looking over the net at the intended target.

My goal in writing this book is to get you to understand the way I approach teaching the game of tennis. I've tried breaking it down in such a way that had it been explained to me this way when I was learning to play the game, I would have thought it would have been very easy to understand how to approach the game and develop the proper technique to make learning the game easier and more fun. In my years of playing tennis, I've read a lot of books and viewed many videos that were in my opinion very helpful but unfortunately too technical and more confusing than helpful to the beginner, recreational, and club player. As an instructor, I am now experiencing the same criticism from my students about tennis instruction books and videos. My attempt is to keep this book on tennis instructions basic and simple, so you can quickly apply it to your practice sessions. It is very easy to get technical. The difficult part I found in reading books on tennis was the pure fact that they were too technical and convoluted to be able to retain the pertinent information that would allow you to apply what you need to learn quickly enough to be able to get out on the tennis court to enjoy the game. However, many instruction parts in this book will apply not only to beginners, but to the highest level player from 5 years of age to 85 years of age. In professional tennis you would be amazed how world-class players will make the same mistakes as club and recreational players but naturally not nearly as often. How many times have you seen your favorite tennis star make the same mistake you make and say to yourself, "Hey that's what I do." So to make it perfectly clear, this book will offer basic factual instruction for all levels of players of any age, in a very easy and simple way. Over the years teaching tennis I've heard some seniors say, "Oh I'm too old to take lessons." I strongly disagree, because I feel it's never too late to learn something new that will benefit you. I have some seniors that have been taking lessons on a regular basis who have improved dramatically. Depending on their ability, and that has a lot to do with my insight on every individual I teach, determines how I approach the lesson the best way for the students to reach their goals. Also, what's important is to always keep in mind your student's objective and to be sure that the student has realistic goals.

In my teaching I use 3 basic objectives I feel make learning to play the game easy and economical and a lot more fun:

1) Freeze your head as you watch the ball at contact
2) Visualize the 'Clock'
3) Overcome Natural Tendencies
*Concentrate, be patient, and most of all have fun.*

# Introduction

## Three Main Objectives of the Book

### Objective 1

**Freezing your head as you watch the ball at contact.**
One of the main objectives or goals I learned early on when I picked up a racket and observed the great Roger Federer and other champions is the old generic term you've heard many many times, "<u>look at the ball.</u>" Looking at the ball is the most important muscle memory you need to learn first and foremost and is not what I see 99.9% tennis players doing, including world-class players, except for a very small percentage.

It wasn't until Roger Federer came on the scene, that freezing your head as you watch the ball at contact was brought to the forefront. Other great champions are obviously hitting the ball very well and have exceptional talent. But, to me, that is why Roger Federer is far superior to the rest and is the greatest tennis player that ever played the game. One of the special attributes of the many he possesses is the ability of keeping his head perfectly still until his stroke is finished before he decides to look over the net at the intended target. This particular reason is why I decided to write an instructional book on tennis. I've studied many tennis pros for years and never have I experienced the expertise of Roger Federer's extraordinary talent of being able to control his head from not moving until his stroke is completely finished. This is one of my main objectives in my teaching. Personal experience has proven how well this works. Couple this with the extraordinary feeling of confidence gained by knowing that if you keep your head still when making contact with the ball you will increase your percentage of keeping the ball in play. Most people, unfortunately including many instructors, think they're looking at the ball; however, in reality they're looking at the intended target across the net and not at the point of contact. In this book, I constantly repeat over and over my concept of what I think is truly looking at the ball. In this book I will make it perfectly clear how to have better focus on the ball. I will also make it perfectly clear how you can improve your eye–hand coordination. Learning how to focus on the ball and having extremely good eye hand coordination, will without a doubt promote a positive attitude and confidence in all your strokes. In my experience teaching tennis, there was hardly a time when one of my students did not say to me, "Wow this is unbelievable how well it works, why haven't I heard this before?" My comment to them is, "Because most tennis instructors themselves are not doing it, and they don't realize they're not doing it because they think they're looking at the ball." In many cases, tennis instructors may feel that other parts of learning the game are more important. I don't feel that way because you can't build the best house in the neighborhood without the best solid foundation. I try to put in simple terms the best possible way to teach the muscle memory in learning to keep your head still as <u>you watch the ball at contact.</u> Because it is without question the most important aspect of the game you should learn <u>first</u> before anything else. I have players that have unorthodox strokes but keep their head so still and look at the ball so incredibly well with such discipline that I've seen them out play players with far better strokes that were technically sound but inconsistent because they could <u>not</u> freeze their head at contact as they watch the ball. You'll also discover greater enjoyment in the game of tennis with major improvements coming rapidly.

In this book you'll find that I offer several alternatives in learning how to develop the muscle memory in what I refer to as **freezing your head** as you watch the ball at contact. I have had a lot of success in my teaching simply because people realize at the moment and on the spot how incredibly well it works when f**reezing your head** as you watch the ball at contact. No matter what level player I've had to teach 99.9% have this common problem. Even though many high-level players I worked with have good technique and play the game very well, they are amazed how much better they instantly play and how fast their level improves by just learning how to look at the ball the best possible way. What many of my students have discovered by developing the muscle memory of looking at the ball the best possible way (and that is **freezing your head** as you watch the ball at contact) is that those hard to get to shots that most likely could end up being an unforced error turnout, at the very least, keeping the ball in play if not becoming an outright winner.

Many students who have come to me and I've asked the simple question, "What is your objective and what can I do to help you ?" All have a variety of reasons from "I need to learn a  particular stroke," to "I don't seem to have enough power," or just a whole series of a bunch of issues. But no one has ever come to me and asked me, "Can you teach me how to look at the ball the best possible way ?" because it's something that most people take for granted simply because they think they are looking at the ball. Even though as I said, we've heard time and time again, "Look at the ball and move your feet," but the reality is most are not looking at the ball the best possible way. In this book, you will definitely learn how to look at the ball the best possible way and discover on the spot instantly  how well it works. Having said that, you could actually get out on the tennis court, without working on your technique first, learn how to **freeze your head** as you watch the ball at contact, which will help you improve and be more consistent instantly with the strokes you already posses. Once you develop this muscle memory everything else will seem easier. But understand this, it makes a lot more sense, and this is something I've learned in my years of teaching, that when someone comes to me for lessons, I let them quickly understand that for me to start teaching them fancy techniques or footwork and talking about different rackets and fancy strings and tensions, is secondary to the #1 objective of learning how to **freeze your head at contact** as you watch the ball. I also will tell them that learning how to **freeze your head at contact** as you watch the ball is very difficult simply because it's a **natural tendency and a normal reaction** to want to look over the net at the intended target. And that's why it could be one of the most difficult parts in learning to play the game of tennis the best possible way. But once you develop this muscle memory, you'll discover you'll have this wonderful and confident feeling that, if you can touch the ball you are going to get the ball back in play. And be honest with yourself, isn't that what the game is all about? In professional tennis most matches are won by their opponent making more unforced errors, unless they are playing exceptional tennis. So, if that's the case at the highest level of tennis, it most definitely pertains to all of us who are not playing at the world-class level.

## Objective 2

**The Clock Theory.** When reading this book you'll be asked to imagine an imaginary clock that might be standing directly in front of you, to either side of you, or on the ground. This hopefully will aid in helping you to learn the proper racket path for developing a particular stroke. I found great success in using this format for all levels of players. The whole point of having a visual such as this imaginary clock seems to be very helpful for most students and also puts in perspective why the stroke works so well. This clock theory, as you'll see, works extremely well on all the strokes. Once you capture the image in your mind, you'll know on your own if you executed the stroke properly. In my experience, at many levels, the beginning to the end of the racket path will explain to you, on your own, why you made an error or not. If you've executed with the proper racket path for a particular stroke you'll see instant success by using the imaginary clock format.

## Objective 3

**Overcoming Natural Tendencies.** Natural tendency is when you do something naturally and/or instinctively without trying. This is a common practice in all tennis players. In my teaching experience, I've discovered that at all levels especially beginners, club, and recreational players have **natural tendencies** that prevent them from playing at a higher level and making less errors. In this book, it is my hope that bringing to your attention the **natural tendencies** on all the strokes and basic strategies will help you correct any **natural tendencies** that are preventing you from improving your technique and consistency and lead to playing a smarter game of tennis. As with the Clock Theory and the muscle memory of Freezing Your Head as you watch the ball at contact, you'll constantly be reminded along with the list of **natural tendencies** for each stroke throughout the book. When you have any questions in regards to the problems you have on a particular stroke, or maybe with technique or just plain all-around errors, you can conveniently look up that particular stroke and skim through the list of the **Natural Tendency List** with the problem you may be having in any given area. This convenient **Natural Tendency List** is there to help you realize the actions you are doing naturally and instinctively without realizing that they could be the cause of your particular problem.

# Grips

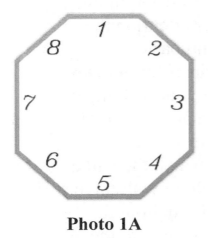

**Photo 1A**

Tennis racquet handles are eight-sided. If the handle was square it would be uncomfortable and may even hurt the hand. If the racket handle was round it would be difficult to grip firmly because there would be no friction. The eight sides on the handle are called bevels. If the blade of the racket is perpendicular to the ground, the bevel facing up is number one.

The one next to it rotating clockwise is number two if you're right-handed and counter clockwise if you are left-handed and so on.

It's commonly said that too large or too small of a grip can cause arm or shoulder problems. In fact, the biggest mistake most people make is gripping the racket too loosely with the wrong fingers. This alone can cause more stress at contact with the racket slipping in your hands. I've usually found players improperly applying more pressure on the racket handle with the thumb, index finger, and middle finger rather than properly with the baby finger, ring finger and middle finger. This is a major cause of the racket moving in your hand at contact. Before you rush to go out and buy a new racket, try applying pressure on the correct fingers first. If you still feel uncomfortable, talk to a USPTA certified professional that can help in choose the correct size that feels right for you.

Gripping the racket handle too tightly promotes stress on your arm, causing you to get tired faster. Naturally, you need to hold the racket handle tight enough so it doesn't move around in your hand or slip out of your hand completely. Apply more pressure with the baby finger, ring finger, and middle finger and not your thumb, index finger and middle finger. You'll have a far more secure grip with more control.

Grip Sizes – from smallest to largest

LO = 4 inches
L1= 41/8 inches
L2= 41/2 inches
L3= 43/8 inches
L4= 41/2 inches
L5= 45/8 inches
L6= 43/4 inches
L7= 47/8 inches
L8=5 inches
Each of the grips described here starts by placing the muscle under the index finger on the bevel number for the desired grip **(see1B and 1C).**

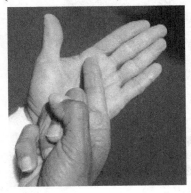

**Photo 1B**

**Photo 1C**

## Grips for Two-Handed
## Backhand Players (Photo1D)

Full Eastern Forehand Grip:
Place muscle under index finger
on the left hand on bevel #7
Full Eastern Backhand Grip:
Place muscle under index
finger on the right hand on bevel
#3

**Photo 1D**

The Continental Grip:
Place muscle under index finger
on the left hand on bevel # 8.
Full Eastern Backhand Grip:
Place muscle under index finger
on the right hand muscle on bevel
#3. **(photo1E)**

**Photo 1E**

Semi-Western Forehand Grip:
Place muscle under index finger on
left hand on bevel # 6.
Semi-Western Backhand Grip:
Place muscle under index finger on
the right hand on bevel #  4.
**(Photo 1F)**

**Photo 1F**

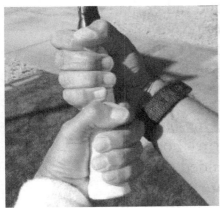

**Photo 1G**

Full Western Forehand Grip: Place muscle under index finger on the left hand on bevel #5. Full Western Backhand Grip: Place muscle under index finger on the right hand on bevel # 5. **(Photo 1G)**

Full Eastern Forehand Grip: Place muscle under index finger on the left hand on bevel # 7. Semi-Western Backhand Grip: Place muscle under index finger on the right hand on bevel # 4. **(Photo1H)**

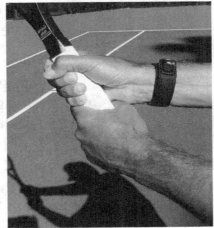

**Photo 1H**

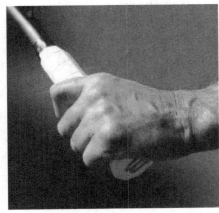

**Photo 1-I**

**Grips for One-Handed Backhand Players (Photo 1-I)** Semi-Western One-Handed Backhand Grip: Place muscle under index finger on left hand on bevel # 2.

This grip is primarily used by one-handed backhand players to hit aggressively over and through their backhand with a great amount of spin 90% of the time. It's also a grip that allows shorter players to hit aggressively over and through their one-handed backhand rather than play more defensively by slicing the ball. The opposite is true for lefties. It is popular with some pros on tour to continually hold the Semi-Western one-handed backhand grip for executing a Semi-Western forehand groundstroke.

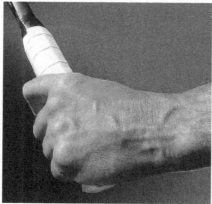

Photo 1J

Full Eastern One-handed Backhand Grip - For left and right one- handed backhand players.**(Photo 1J)**

Place muscle under index finger on right-hand on Bevel #1. This grip is primarily used for the one-handed backhand drive. A Full Eastern Backhand Grip is used by one-handed backhand players who prefer to come over their backhand the majority of the time. It is also used at times to hit a kick serve because it puts the racket angle on the ball that makes it easier to impart more spin.  It's also used by some players to slice their backhand.

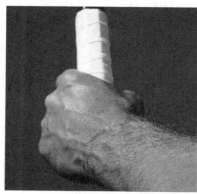

Photo 1K

Continental Grip – For right-handed players.**(Photo 1K)**

Place muscle under index finger on left hand on Bevel # 8. This grip is used for the backhand drive, serve, overhead smash, volley, backhand slice, forehand slice, drop shot, and occasionally forehand roundstrokes. This grip is also used to assist the

left hand (dominant hand) for the two-handed backhand.
The Continental Grip is applied by placing the muscle under your index finger on your left hand on Bevel #8 for left-handed players.

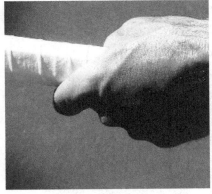

(Photo 1-L)

Grips for **Forehand** Groundstroke
<u>Full Eastern Forehand Grip:</u>  For right-handed and left-handed.
**(Photo 1-L)**
Place muscle under index finger on the left hand on Bevel # 7. This grip is mainly used for the forehand groundstroke but can be used for the serve, overhead smash, and forehand volley. For right-handed players the muscle under the index finger on the right hand would be applied to Bevel # 3. It will be used at times for two-handed backhand players or two-handed forehand players. The Full Eastern Forehand Grip will sometimes be used for volleys, serves, and the overhead smash by lower level players because it puts the angle of the racket on the ball in a comfortable position.

The Full Eastern Forehand Grip is the most adaptable and versatile grip. It allows you to hit very high-bouncing balls aggressively with spin, flat, or slice, and low-bouncing balls with spin or slice on various surfaces. It's also a grip that feels natural for most players, especially beginners. This grip is sometimes used to hit volleys, serves, and the overhead smash for those players who find holding the Continental Grip unnatural.

Semi-Western Forehand Grip: For right-handed and left-handed players.(**Photo 1M** )

Place muscle under index finger on left hand on Bevel # 6. This grip is used to produce a great amount of spin. For right-handed players the muscle under the index finger

**(Photo 1M)**

would be applied to Bevel # 4, primarily for the forehand groundstroke to impart spin. For two-handed backhand groundstrokes use the right hand to hold the Semi-Western grip for left-handed players, opposite for right-handed players.

Same as with the Full Western Forehand Grip, some players on the ATP tour prefer to hold the Semi-Western Grip to hit a one-handed backhand (Bevel # 2) for economical reasons, simply because the exchange on groundstrokes are returning too fast. Some pros find it helpful for returning serve. That grip is now called a Semi-Western Backhand Grip (bevel # 2).

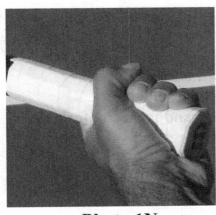

**Photo 1N**

<u>Full Western Forehand Grip:</u> For right and left-handed players. Place muscle under index finger on left hand on Bevel #5. **(Photo 1N)**

This grip is used for forehand groundstrokes to produce a tremendous amount of spin and help shorter players return high bouncing balls. Some pros on the tour find it economical to hold a Full Western Grip to hit a one-handed backhand. Hitting a one-handed backhand the grip is now called a Full Eastern Backhand Grip – Bevel #1. Some players will change from a Full Western Forehand Grip to a Full Eastern Backhand Grip instinctively, if they play a one-handed backhand. This grip is also used with two-handed backhand groundstrokes, allowing the right hand to hold the Full Western Forehand Grip, while the left hand is holding either a Continental Grip Bevel #8 or a Full Eastern Forehand Grip Bevel #7.

# Forehand

The forehand is by far the most natural stroke in the game of tennis. The majority in a tennis match will be hit by the forehand groundstroke. Players will go as far as running around their backhand just to hit a forehand. Since the forehand feels comfortable and natural, learning to be consistent with the forehand is a wise approach to playing the game.

Once you have learned to control the forehand by being consistent, you gain confidence by using the stroke as a weapon.

**Photo 1A**

**There are several forms of the forehand from basic to advanced.**

**Closed Stance (or Square Stance)**
This stance is the most natural for beginners to adapt. With your racket positioned in front of your chest just below your chin, step in and across toward the net with your right foot for left-handed players. Opposite for righties. **(Photo 1A)**

**Semi-Open Stance**
This more advanced stance is normally used by higher-level players incorporating the angular momentum technique - (the rotation of your hips and shoulders during contact with your left shoulder facing the net at the duration of the stroke). You step across toward the alley, loading up with your weight on your left leg for left-handed players. **(Photo 1B)**

**Photo 1B**

**Open Stance**

For this stance, you bring your left leg up in line - shoulder-width apart - with your right leg so your chest and belly face the net when making contact with the ball. Opposite for righties. **(Photo 1C)**

**Photo 1C**

## The 3 L's

For more advanced students the mechanics normally used for the Elevated, Vertical, Horizontal and the Inverted Forehand groundstrokes are achieved by incorporating the **3 L's** technique.

**L-1** is facing the fence behind you toward the sky above your head with your elbow remaining elevated or level with your left shoulder as you prepare to take the racket back. **(Photo 1D)**

**Photo 1D**

**L-2** is facing the fence behind you but lower and somewhat level with the oncoming ball with the hitting surface of the racket facing the ground. L-2 is also part

**Photo 1E**

of the forehand ground stroke that incorporates the flip. The flip starts with the butt of the racket handle aiming toward the ball with a laid back wrist, then snapping your wrist just before making contact

**Photo 1F**

with the ball. **(Photo 1E)**
**L-3** is the contact point. This is where it's crucial for you to keep your head perfectly still *as if you're posing for a picture as you make contact with the ball* with a 10° closed racket (facing the ground) on the ball. Pronate as you brush up the backside of the ball at contact. **(Photo 1F)**

## Strokes

**The Elevated Forehand** - grip of choice: Eastern Forehand

The Elevated is the most common and natural stroke for the forehand. The stroke ends up across your body above your opposite shoulder as if to scratch your back. One of the best ways to visualize this stroke is to imagine an imaginary clock *standing*

*directly in front of you.* Think of the path of the racquet swinging low to high from 7 o'clock up and across the imaginary clock to 1 o'clock and over your opposite shoulder as if to scratch your back. For righties - 5 to 11.

**The Vertical Forehand** - grips of choice: Eastern, Semi-Western, and Full Western

The nature of the vertical stroke imparts spin. With this stroke the path of the racquet goes from low to high and starts and ends on the same side of your body. This stroke is also known as the Reverse Forehand. To visualize this stroke, go back to that imaginary clock *standing directly in front of you.* The path of this stroke for your racquet goes from 7 o'clock up to 11 o'clock. For righties – 5 to 1.

**The Horizontal Forehand** - grips of choice: Eastern, Semi-Western, and Full Western

Position your racquet perpendicular to the ground to allow you to hit flat or with topspin and drive through the middle of the ball aggressively. The path of the racquet starts and ends on the same level across your body. This works best on high balls that are above the net, allowing you to hit with more down force to drive the ball in a straight line with tremendous pace. A ball that is hit without spinning travels through the air faster than a ball with spin, providing the path of the ball is traveling high to low in a straight downward motion. 10 to 2 or 9 to 3

**The Inverted Forehand** - grips of choice: Eastern, Semi-Western and Full Western

The Inverted Forehand is known as the windshield wiper stroke - low to high and back to low. It is the most popular stroke with tennis pros. It produces a tremendous amount of spin along with greater access to better angles. It can be incorporated from any part of the court with pace and still keep the ball within the lines. This stroke is most beneficial with very low approach shots.

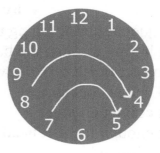

With the imaginary clock *standing directly in front of you*, the path of the racquet goes from 7 o'clock up, across and down to 5 o'clock or from 8 o'clock up, across and down to 4 o'clock. Opposite for right-handed players. The path of the racquet resembles a half moon. On very low balls, **face the hitting surface toward the net through the finish on the stroke**. The hitting surface will be facing the same direction as the palm of your hand. If you attempt to come over the ball your chances of hitting into the net are greater.

Facing the hitting surface toward the net at all times through contact as you brush up the backside of the ball will impart top spin and lessen the chance of hitting the ball into the net. It's as if you're putting the racquet in your pocket at the end of the stroke.

## Frequently Asked Questions

### Why do I keep hitting my forehand into the net, wide, late, long, and have too many miss-hits?

1) Not freezing your head as you make contact with the ball.
2) Using the wrong grip.
3) Bringing your back shoulder around too soon.
4)  Finishing incorrectly on follow-through.
5) Not hitting through the ball at contact.
6) Not having the racquet back facing the fence behind you early enough.
7) Hitting under the ball at contact.
8) Swinging full speed from six o'clock to three o'clock.
9) Too late at contact.
10) Racquet not in front of you in ready position.
11) Racquet head speed varies too much.
12) Miss hits.

### Why do I lack power?

1) Racquet not back facing the fence behind you early enough.
2) Not hitting through the ball.
3) Incorrect finish on follow-through.
4) Too late at contact.
5) Not coiling enough.
6) Not enough racquet head speed.
7) Poor timing
8) Incorrect technique.
9) Not staying down at contact.

# Why am I inconsistent and lack control?

1) Swinging full speed from 6 o'clock to 9 o'clock.
2) Miss hits.
3) Not staying down at contact.
4) Not hitting through the ball at contact.
5) The wrong grip.
6) Racquet not back facing the fence behind you early enough.
7) Finishing incorrectly on follow-through.
8) Too late at contact.
9) Not having racquet in front of you in the ready position.

## How do I improve my forehand to the next level?

1) Freeze your head as you watch the ball at contact.
2) Hit at the apex or on the rise.
3) Don't wait for the ball to come to you, go to the ball.
4) Stay down at contact.
5) Learn to maintain steady racquet head speed to stay in a rally.
6) Learn to hit with more power by developing the combination of proper technique, excellent timing, and tremendous racquet head speed.

## How do I get more power on my forehand?

Combination of proper technique, excellent timing, and tremendous racquet head speed.

## Why does my racquet keep slipping and turning in my hand?

Your grip should be more secure with the baby finger, ring finger, and middle finger, as opposed to the thumb, index finger, and middle finger.

## Overcoming Natural Tendencies

### Not freezing your head as you watch the ball at contact.

There are several ways to help you learn to keep your head still when watching the ball at contact. **First way:** look for the blur of the racquet head through the contact zone. You'll see just a trail or a blur of the racquet head going through the hitting zone. If you don't see it, that means you are looking over the net at the intended target. Once you've developed this muscle memory, you'll become confident that if you can touch the ball you're going to get it back in

play. Freezing your head as you watch the ball at contact is like posing for a picture. **(Photo 1G)** When you do it correctly, you should see the ball for the first time when it is passing over the net and not on your side of the court. Pose when making contact and look over the net when you finish the stroke. If you look up too soon you'll be assuming you're looking at the ball. It's a major natural tendency and a common problem. **Second way:** your chin should end up resting on your left shoulder as you finish the stroke.

**Photo 1G**                    **Third way:** concentrate on the color of the ball at the point of contact. You'll find it is so much easier to track the ball on courts that are part sun and shade. Trying to follow the ball in and out of the sun and shade can be difficult for even the top players in the world. It requires a lot of concentration. **Fourth way:** finish the stroke first then look over the net regardless of the style of your stroke. **The fifth effective way** is to think of how most tennis courts are designed to go north to south. When you make contact with the ball on your groundstrokes and volleys, your chin should be facing east or west. Despite the direction, a good concept is to imagine your chin should be facing towards the alleys during contact.

## Moving your head at the point of contact
## when running down a ball

As you run down a ball try to freeze your head as you watch the ball at contact. Try not to worry about placement or even where your opponent is. What's important is **where you saw your opponent last**. Think of an airline pilot. They're not looking out a windshield, they're reading their gauges. The racquet head is your gauge, and looking at the intended target as you hit the ball will not help as much as focusing on the ball in the contact zone.

## Not having racquet back facing the fence behind
## you before the ball bounces in front of you

It's been said that getting the racquet back too early disrupts the natural rhythm. For some that may be the case, but I'd rather see the racquet back too early than too late. The key to good preparation is having the racquet back facing the fence behind you just before the ball bounces in front of you. Be sure not to have a hitch in your stroke. Don't stop in the middle of your swing. I see players getting their racquets back to 6 o'clock too slowly only having to rush forward to hit the ball at the contact point (9 o'clock). The racquet should be back quickly to 6 o'clock and forward to 9 o'clock slowly and smoothly (for left-handed players). Opposite for righties would be from 6 to 3. Not only will your timing be better but you'll find it feels good on your arm because the contact point will be made out in front of you. Also, you'll have your body behind the ball instead of the ball behind your body. It will feel smoother and you'll be more relaxed.

## Having the racquet hanging down the side of your leg

This makes it far more difficult to time the ball at the proper contact point out in front of your body, **(Photo 1H)**. Furthermore it makes it far more difficult to time it correctly to hit a backhand. We've heard

**Photo 1H**

so many times to have the racquet up in the ready position vertically just below our chin and in front of your chest. I agree and especially for two-handed backhand players **(Photo 1-I)**. As correct as this may be, the game of tennis has become more powerful and faster and players on the pro tour have become bigger and stronger and technology has made it possible for club and recreational players to hit with more power with less effort. But for one-handed backhand players, having the racquet in a vertical ready position is not as economical as having your racquet at waist height positioned across your body from left to right with the head positioned directly in front or just above your right hip. **(Photo 1J.)** Opposite for right-handed players. With your racquet in this position you have more options by relying on your backhand because the joint in your arm allows you to move in all directions without moving your feet. This works well on volleys and the return of serve on the backhand side, because backhands have a tendency to be late more often than forehands. With the racquet position across your body in front of you at waist height or just above, you'll have more time returning on the backhand side. You'll see a difference in how much time you have to react by relying on the backhand volley more than the forehand volley. For two- handed backhand players I recommend having the racquet in ready position below your chin in front of your chest vertically.

| Photo 1I | Photo 1J |

## Not playing enough angles

For most of us the natural tendency is to walk out on a tennis court and instinctively want to hit the ball hard. By utilizing angles you force your opponent to move to the ball. When you play against someone with poor mobility it becomes easier to force them to feel rushed and your chances for an unforced error or hitting an out-right winner are greater. Your objective should be for your opponent to move more than you. An important point to remember is the net is lower in the middle at 3 feet as opposed to 3.5 feet in the alley. Hitting angled shots over the lower part of the net gives you a smaller margin for error. Learning to hit great angles takes time away from your opponent to get in place. When you hit your groundstrokes at the apex you'll have better access to more angles and options.

## Waiting for the ball to descend

It's a natural tendency to wait for the ball to come to you. When you do you are letting the ball play you. You're putting yourself in the position of waiting for the ball to descend while it's dropping from its highest point. The game of tennis is about <u>Time, Place, Angles, and Options</u>. Hitting the ball at the apex gives you an edge and a big advantage to hit it earlier and more aggressively. Taking the ball at the top of the bounce takes time away from your opponent getting into place. Taking the ball at the top of the bounce usually means the contact point is above the net. That will allow you the opportunity to drive through the shot. Also, when making contact at the apex you have access to better angles and more options. The other advantage is the opportunity to impart the horizontal ground stroke, which means the path of your racquet will go from 10 o'clock across to 2 o'clock.

## Foot Work -Weight on the wrong foot (Back Foot)

Having the weight on the back foot can result in poor balance and can be the cause of lack of power and consistency. Typically, leaning back is the cause for not moving to left or right from the incoming ball and not preparing quickly enough so you can adjust your body weight forward to the ball. Not moving to the ball will catch you off guard and off balance, thus you find yourself hitting off the back foot. There will be times when you will be forced to hit off the back

**Photo 1K**

foot because the ball comes back too fast and deep. This is normal. When confronted with a ball that is deep with pace, try to resist moving back away from the ball. Stand your ground and hit the ball

on the rise. Most importantly be prepared to freeze your head as you watch the ball at contact. That will make hitting the ball on the rise much easier. **(Photo 1K)**

## Jumping up when hitting groundstrokes

We see the pros lifting off the ground when hitting their groundstrokes so it's natural for some of us to want to emulate them. The fact is you're witnessing their natural momentum lifting them up due to the pace, depth, and position of the ball at the moment. The best players are the ones not lifting off the ground as much because once you elevate off the ground your racquet head is lifting with you. When that happens it's far more difficult to have control of your shots. What you want to do is stay down through the shot moving horizontally not vertically, so you have more control through the contact point consistently. For the best results don't try to emulate your favorite tennis star by lifting off the ground just because it looks cool. Stay down through the stroke for control and let the natural momentum lift you.

## Racquet head speed varies too much

Learning to have control in the speed of the racquet head will help tremendously in keeping the ball in play in a rally. By swinging too fast then swinging too slowly when you're rushing, you end up swinging very fast and slapping at the ball and sacrificing control. Concentrating on the bounce helps get the racquet back at 6 o'clock (facing the fence behind you) just before the ball bounces in front of you. This helps you prepare early enough with a smooth and fluid motion without a hitch so it's easier to time the ball at 9 o'clock (contact point) to make contact in front of your front foot. Think of the imaginary clock *on the ground and you're standing in the middle of it*. With your racquet facing the fence behind you for early preparation at 6 o'clock, your racquet head acceleration should actually start to pick up speed at the **control zone** between 8 o'clock and 9 o'clock. If you are a righty your racquet head acceleration will

pick up at the **control zone** from 4 o'clock to make contact at 3 o'clock. You are picking up racquet head speed just before making contact with the ball. The key is to keep the racquet head speed the same as much as possible for being consistent enough to stay in the rally. When attempting to hit a winner to end the point, accelerate the racquet head with greater velocity at the **control zone** just before you are ready to make contact with the ball from 8 o'clock to 9 o'clock.

## Hitting under the ball

Most beginners and players at the club and recreational level have the tendency to hit under the ball with the racquet face slanted up facing the sky. In other words, they're making contact with an open racquet face. Naturally you end up hitting balls that float and result in your shots being too high over the net and going long. This is better known as "moon balls."

One of the easiest ways to fix this problem is to simply think of hitting directly behind the ball or with a 10° racquet angle on the ball facing the ground. (**Photo 1L**)

**Photo 1L**

When you have your racquet closed at 10° on the ball, you're actually hitting down. As you hit down on the ball you have to be sure to finish up and across to 1 o'clock (across the right shoulder). If you don't finish up as you hit down the ball, you'll end up hitting over the top of the ball causing you to hit into the net or the ground. By hitting up and across the ball with the racquet at 10° angle facing down on the ball, you will be hitting with (**Photo 1M**) topspin and driving the ball. This also helps to keep the ball lower and closer to the net as opposed to more height over the net.

## Racquet keeps slipping and turning in hand

You are holding the racquet tighter with the wrong fingers - the thumb, index finger, and middle finger. Holding the racquet with the little finger, ring finger, and middle finger tighter will give you the secured grip needed to stop the racquet from turning and slipping in your hand. You'll find this works well even with a grip that's worn out and/or sweaty.

**Photo 1M**

## Hitting up and across too early

This results in hitting into the net, hitting wide or just being inconsistent. At contact hit through the ball as far as your arm can reach toward the net, then go up and across your opposite (right) shoulder as if to scratch your back from 7 o'clock to 1 o'clock . If you are a righty go up and across to the opposite (left) shoulder from 5 to 11. Hitting up and across too early requires a lot more racquet head acceleration to get the ball over the net as opposed to hitting out. Hitting out means to extend your hitting arm out toward the net as far as you can reach as you make contact with the ball. This exaggerated motion ensures that you'll have full extension before you go up and across the opposite shoulder to complete the stroke. It's more important to learn to hit out rather than up and across prematurely.

# Contact point too far back

Photo 1N (head still)

Photo 1P (head not still)

Contact point too far back results in a lack of power, hitting long or hitting moon balls. Concentrating on where the ball bounces in front of you will make it easier to make contact in front of your front foot. You'll have your arm and body behind the ball with a laid-back wrist for better leverage. When you're making contact in front of your body it's easier to see the ball. With great concentration follow the ball off your opponent's racquet. As the ball is coming over the net, track it closely to focus on where it's going to bounce and make contact in front of your front foot so your body and your fully extended arm will be completely behind the ball. Or, you can think of the hitting point as an imaginary wall where you want to make contact with the ball. Doing this helps step into the shot by getting your body weight forward to achieve more power. Your racquet will be squared off in such a way that you'll find yourself hitting behind the ball rather than under the ball which will result in hitting moon balls. **Photo 1N**, contact point too far back, but looking at the ball. **Photo 1P**, contact point too far back and not looking at the ball.

## Not playing the ball

Most people will wait for the ball to come to them. Tennis is a game of <u>Time, Place, Angles, and Options.</u> Waiting for the ball to come to you will only make you end up hitting up and over the net which gives your opponent more time to get to the ball. The better choice is to hit the ball at the apex, which would usually be higher than the net and allow you to hit directly through the ball with tremendous down force and more authority in a straight line. Hitting down into the court takes time away from your opponent getting into position to hit the ball. Instead of the ball going over the net in an arc with a lot of height, the ball will travel over the net with a lower arc in more of a downward motion more aggressively in a straight line in the form of a missile. By hitting at the apex your options are greater because you have more angles available to hit into the court. Think about it, if you were in a fight and you were on the bottom you would have the disadvantage of having to hit up, but if you were on top you would have the distinct advantage because you would be hitting down with far more down force. You want to be hitting down on the ball with more authority so you can drive it with some spin. If you find hitting the ball at the apex is difficult for you, then by all means hitting the ball when it descends is perfectly acceptable and is not wrong.

## Not realizing there are options

It's a natural tendency in the heat of the moment to want to rush to the ball as quickly as possible. At that moment you react by just hitting it and not considering that other options exist. You could, for example, hit a low volley instead of letting the ball bounce or wait for the ball to reach its apex so you could hit a more aggressive shot such as a horizontal groundstroke that would drive the ball. Other options may include a drop shot or maybe a shot that allows you to hit greater angles when you hit at the top of the bounce. Stay relaxed and control your emotions when rushing to the ball and understand you have other options. This is much easier said than done but by hitting lots of balls it will start to become instinctive if you maintain that mindset. In some cases your option could be to hit the shot to your opponent closest to the net who can't react quickly enough and not to their partner who is further away and who has more time to react. This is a very common mistake I see every day. Try to stay relaxed and this will help tremendously in making the right decision at the right moment.

## Not using right arm to push racquet back

In most cases early preparation includes bringing the racquet back quickly to 6 o'clock (facing the fence behind you) to come forward slowly and smoothly to the **control zone** from 8 o'clock to 9 o'clock (contact point). Using your right arm to push the racquet back will help you turn by coiling your shoulders - turning your shoulders sideways to the net enough so your opponent can actually see your back. Doing this helps you completely uncoil into the shot which in turn helps you generate more power in your strokes more efficiently with less effort.

## Hitting the ball with underspin

The problem with hitting underspin is air is rushing under the ball which makes the ball float, causing your groundstrokes to go long. If I tell a beginner I'm going to feed them balls and ask them to hit without thinking, 9 out of 10 times they will chop down or slap at the ball with natural underspin. **(Photo 1R)** A good way to learn more control is to hit out and through on the ball at the same time your racquet path is moving from low to high. Thinking of the clock theory, *(the imaginary clock standing directly in front of you),* the swing path of the racquet would travel from 7 o'clock up and across your body to 1 o'clock as if to scratch your back .That will instantly stop you from chopping down on the ball and make you hit through the stroke giving you more of an offensive shot by adding topspin or hitting the ball flat. When your racquet head is in the position for

contact, think of the <u>top of the frame leading first</u> with the bottom of the racquet head to follow. **(Photo 1Q)** This will prevent you from hitting under the ball with an open racquet (facing the sky) but will also help in hitting with some topspin along with driving your shot by making contact directly through the middle of the ball. A common mistake with most beginners, club, or recreational players, is that when the racquet is back facing the fence behind you at 6 o'clock, the racquet face is

**Photo 1Q**

slightly open facing the sky. For better results you want your racquet face facing down towards the ground. By the time you make contact in front of your body your racquet head will be at a 10° angle facing the ground hitting with more down-force to impart topspin along with driving the ball. Another good solution is having the mindset to have your racquet perpendicular to the ground at contact to hit flat through the ball.

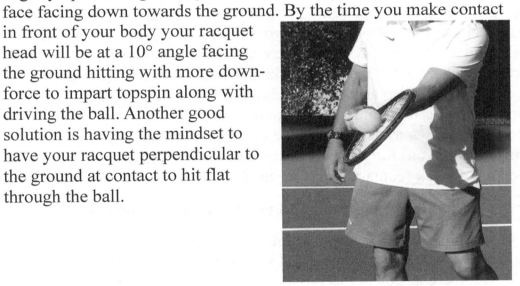

**Photo 1R**

## Stroking up and across too early

This is <u>very</u> common at most levels. Strive to hit out through the ball first and then finish up and across. It's more important to learn to hit out than it is to hit up and across. Hitting up and across requires more racquet head speed to get the ball over the net as opposed to hitting out. Hitting out, up and across is good for hitting with more depth. Hitting out extends your racquet arm through the contact point toward the net as far as you can reach before you decide to go up and across your body to the opposite shoulder. If you can exaggerate this motion, it will help you to learn to extend out through the hitting zone. Along with pace and depth this will also help you to be more consistent.

## Not having racquet back when running down a ball

The natural tendency when running down a ball is to have the racquet in front of you. As you run have the racquet back to 6 o'clock (facing the fence behind you) so when you are in position to make contact out in front of your front foot, you will be prepared to swing forward smoothly with more control in the **control zone** (from 8 o'clock to 9 o'clock) to make contact at 9 o'clock (contact point). This is called a running forehand. Pete Sampras was famous for his running forehand. In order to do this efficiently and economically, your racquet must be back at 6 o'clock (facing the fence behind you) for you to time the ball out in front of your front foot at 9 o'clock (contact point) for the best results.

## With a Running Forehand you have Three Choices:

1) Get there as quickly as possible to give yourself time to set up and get your balance to get your weight moving forward.
2) Get there as quickly as possible but as you approach the ball slow down by using little steps as you keep moving through the ball.
3) If you're late getting there, you have no other choice but to run through the shot at a full sprint.

## Miss hits

This is a common problem I see mostly at the beginner, club, and recreational levels. The best cure is to think of that imaginary clock *that is on the ground and you're standing in the middle of it.* Imagine accelerating your racquet just before making contact with the ball from 8 o'clock to 9 o'clock, **(control zone)** and not from 6 o'clock to 9 o'clock. By having this mindset you will have a better chance of hitting the sweet spot as opposed to swinging full speed from 6 o'clock to 9 o'clock (contact point). With your full concentration on the **control zone,** you'll have less miss hits.

## Lack of power

To develop power for your forehand you must have proper technique along with good timing and tremendous racquet head speed. Part of the proper technique involves your racquet being closed at 10° on the ball at contact swinging low to high. Your contact point must be made in front of your front foot so as to have your arm and body behind the ball. And just before contact a tremendous amount of racquet speed is required. For more power you need good timing, lots of racquet head speed, and the proper technique.

# Backhand

There are three ways to execute Backhands: Under Spin (also called Slice), Topspin, and Flat. The most natural of the three is the Under Spin. Someone who has never held a racquet will naturally strike the ball with under spin without realizing it. It's a natural motion for one-handed backhand players. The most difficult is the topspin one-handed backhand drive. Because our left arm by nature is already in front of our body, as we turn sideways in position to the net it's easy to be late if we don't time it just right. For two-handed backhand players the contact point is not quite as far out in front of the front foot as with the one-handed backhand. When one-handed backhand players are a little late, the ball can easily get behind the striking zone resulting in the shot spraying wide to the right.

## The One-Handed Backhand Groundstroke

Unlike the forehand ground stroke, the one-handed backhand ground stroke is an unnatural motion for most people. The forehand groundstroke resembles a side arm throwing motion. The one-handed backhand is more like the feeling of pulling. Having problems with the one-handed backhand is not at all unusual. World-class pros practice for years to perfect their one-handed backhand. Many players choose to run around their one-handed backhand to hit a forehand. Doing this only delays the ultimate goal of being confident of the stroke. The payoff for practicing your one-handed backhand is it will end up being as reliable as your forehand.

The grip of choice for the one-handed backhand is the Full Eastern Backhand grip. With this grip you now have your whole hand and arm behind the ball for better leverage. You can think of it as adjusting the first knuckle just at the bottom of your index finger so it's on top of bevel 1 on the racquet handle. Take the palm of your hand and put it directly on the top of bevel 1 close to the end of the racquet handle.

Early preparation is very important. It enables you to meet the ball out in front of your front foot. What you want is to make contact with a racquet head at a closed 10° angle on the ball with the racquet angled towards the ground. As counter intuitive as it may sound, you have to hit down on the ball with down force. As you do so, you will be brushing up the back side of the ball at a 10° angle. Hit out through the ball extending your arm toward the net as far as you can reach as you brush up and across, finish the stroke above and in front of your right shoulder. As you make contact with the ball try to envision the *imaginary clock that* is *directly in front of you.* The path of the racquet will go from 5 o'clock up and across to 11 o'clock almost like tossing a Frisbee. Most importantly, as you make contact with the ball, freeze your head. Use your right arm to pull the racquet back and turn your shoulders to coil so you can uncoil into the shot.

**Photo 2A**

Coil enough so that your opponent can see your back when you bring your racquet back facing the fence behind you at 6 o'clock. **(Photo 2A)**

**Photo 2B**

As you make contact with the ball resist squaring off your shoulders to the net too soon. Imagine holding your profile to the net as you make contact with the ball until the stroke is finished. Try to stay sideways to the net and let the natural momentum pull your right shoulder around naturally so your chest and belly ultimately face the net. If you open your shoulders too early or uncoil too prematurely, chances are you will lose control and end up spraying the ball wide, long, or into the net. **(Photo 2B)**

As you bring your racquet forward to make contact with the ball, exchange your weight from your back foot to your front foot to step into the ball. You want your body weight going forward in the direction of the target. Be very sure that you stay <u>down</u> as you make contact with the ball. A common problem is to lift up as you make contact. When you lift up your racquet head lifts. Stay down until you finish the stroke and you'll have more control in your shots.

### The 3 L's

Racquet towards the back fence pointing up to the sky above the head.
**Photo 2C**

Racquet facing the back fence at 6 o'clock roughly waist height preparing to come forward with the butt of the handle leading first.
**Photo 2D**

The contact point well out in front of the front foot with arm extended straight with the racquet head at a 10° angle closed on the ball facing the ground for topspin.
**Photo 2E**

### The One-Handed Backhand Slice

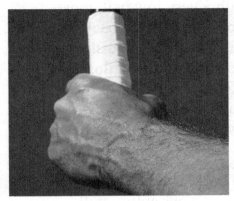

**Photo 2F**

When hitting a one-handed backhand slice the grip of choice is the Continental Grip.**(Photo 2F)**

With the imaginary clock *on the ground and you're standing in the middle of it*, be sure your racquet preparation is at 6 o'clock before the ball bounces in front of you, so you can time it properly at 3 o'clock. Freeze Your Head as you watch the ball at contact. The path of the racquet for the slice will go from 5 o'clock to 10 o'clock, or 4 o'clock to 10 o'clock. Remain sideways to the net until you finish the stroke. If you lift your head too soon to look at the intended target, your shoulders square off or lift up and you lose control of the stroke.

**Photo 2G**

For some people finishing the slice up appears to be more difficult than finishing in a horizontal manner. This is perfectly acceptable providing that as you watch the ball at contact you continue to freeze your head and remain sideways to the net as you hit out through the ball. **(Photo 2G).** The other most common mistake is lifting up as you make contact with the ball on ground strokes. When confronted with a high bouncing ball to your one handed backhand, the only option is to chop or chip down on the back side of the ball to keep the ball in play.

There are three occasions when I believe you should slice your one-handed backhand. **First**, when the ball is too high outside your hitting zone. **Second**, when you are late or out of position and need to buy time to get back into position. **Third**, if you just want to change up the rhythm. When confronted with a very low ball, most tennis instructors will advise you to slice your one-handed backhand because there is less chance of making a mistake. When you slice the ball you are actually playing defensively, as opposed to coming over the ball more offensively. It is far more difficult to come over the ball the majority of the time on your one-handed backhand as opposed to slicing it, but in the long-run it will make you a far better player.

I'm not saying that slicing your one-handed backhand is wrong. I am a strong believer in having as many weapons as your ability will allow. But if you want to play at the highest level, coming over the ball will make you more dangerous by having that weapon in your backhand arsenal. You need to accept it <u>in your mind first</u> in order for it to translate down to your racquet and develop the muscle memory needed to do it instinctively. Otherwise, you will constantly be playing your one-handed backhand defensively by slicing the stroke the majority of the time.

# Frequently Asked Questions

## Why Do I keep hitting into the net, wide, late, long or miss-hits?

One of the main reasons is not freezing your head as you watch the ball at contact. If you constantly hit into the net, you are lifting your head and not hitting out through the contact zone. If you hit late, your racquet is not back early enough facing the fence behind you. If your shots are long, you could be hitting under the ball, instead of hitting with a 10° closed racquet angle down on the ball for topspin. One of the main reasons for miss hits is moving your head as you make contact with the ball and not accelerating the racquet head from 4 o'clock to 3 o'clock in the control zone.

## What grip do I hold?

The Full Eastern Backhand grip or the Semi-Western Backhand grip for topspin. Continental grip for slicing (for one handed backhand players).

## Why do I lack power?

1) Holding the wrong grip (forehand grip).
2) Racquet not back early enough.
3) Not hitting through the ball at contact.
4) Incorrect finish on follow-through.
5) Hitting too late at contact.
6) Not coiling enough.
7) Slicing backhand the majority of the time.
8) Not having racquet in front of you in ready position.
9) Not staying down at contact.
10) Incorrect technique.
11) Poor timing.
12) Not enough racquet head speed.

## Why am I inconsistent and lack control?

1) Swinging full speed from 6 o'clock to 3 o'clock.
2) Running around your backhand to hit a forehand.
3) Miss- hits.
4) Not staying down at contact.
5) Not hitting through the ball at contact.
6) Holding the wrong grip (forehand grip).
7) Racquet not back early enough.
8) Incorrect finish on follow-through.
9) Hitting too late at contact.
10) Not having racquet in front of you in ready position.
11) Last but not least, moving your head when making contact with the ball.

## How do I improve my one-handed backhand to the next level?

1) Freeze your head as you watch the ball at contact as if you are posing for a picture.
2) Hit at the apex or on the rise.
3) Don't wait for the ball to come to you.
4) Stay down at contact.
5) Learn to maintain a steady racquet head speed to stay in a rally for consistency.
6) Don't run around your backhand to hit a forehand.
7) Hit over your backhand the majority of the time instead of slicing.
8) Practice, practice, practice!

## How do I get more power with of my one-handed backhand?

1) Tremendous racquet head speed.
2) Proper timing.
3) Proper technique.

## Overcoming Natural Tendencies
## One Handed Backhand
### Not freezing your head at contact when watching the ball

**Photo 2H**

It's a normal reaction to want to look up over the net at your intended target at the same time you are making contact with the ball. Freezing your head as you watch the ball at contact will quickly raise your level of confidence. The ball will appear as big as a baseball once you start disciplining yourself to keep your head still as if posing for a picture. Think of how most tennis courts are designed north to south. Your chin should be facing east or west or the alleys when making contact with the ball for your backhand. **(Photo 2H)**

### Holding the incorrect grip

Players forget to change their grip from forehand to backhand. With the improper grip, you cause all the shock at contact to travel up your arm which can easily develop into tennis elbow. Place the muscle at the bottom of your index finger on top of the racquet handle. With this grip (the Full Eastern Backhand) you'll have the palm of your hand on top of the

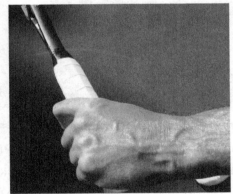

**Photo 2-I**

racquet handle with your whole hand and arm behind the racquet for better leverage at contact. **(Photo 2-I)**

Shock starts at the wrist. By securing your wrists with some form of wrist band, you stop the impact there so it doesn't travel up your arm.

## Not staying sideways during contact

Once making contact with the ball, resist the temptation to bring your back shoulder around too soon to face the net.**(Photo 2J )** Not

only will squaring your shoulders to the net prematurely cause you to move your head, it will also prevent you from controlling the shot. If you coil enough for your opponent to see your back, you will generate plenty of power by uncoiling and stepping into the shot staying sideways through the finish. Let your momentum carry your back shoulder around naturally for more control.

**Photo 2J**

## Incorrect finish on the follow-through

**Photo 2K**                                   **Photo 2L**

Whether your swing starts at 5 o'clock or 4 o'clock or even 3 o'clock, finish <u>up</u> and <u>across</u> your body at 11 o'clock.

Incorrect follow-through - 5 o'clock <u>across</u> and <u>down</u> to 8 o'clock or 7 o'clock. **See Photo 2L**

Correct follow-through - 5 o'clock, or 4 o'clock, or 3 o'clock <u>up</u> and <u>across</u> to 11 o'clock.  **See Photo 2K.**

## Not hitting through the ball at contact

Avoid coming up and across the ball prematurely instead of hitting out through the contact zone. Keep moving the racquet forward toward the net in the direction you want the ball to travel until you can't reach any further. Think in terms of aiming for the baseline. Hitting out through the shot gives you a better chance of getting the ball over the net.

## Racquet not back early enough

Make sure the racquet is facing the fence behind you at 6 o'clock just before the ball bounces in front of you. This will help you keep a continuous motion in your stroke and will help your timing and control. The common problem with most players is getting the racquet back too slowly and having to rush forward in an effort to hit the ball. You want the exact opposite. *With the imaginary clock on the ground and you standing in the middle of it,* your racquet should be back facing the back fence behind you at 6 o'clock with enough time for you to swing forward slowly and smoothly to make contact in the **control zone** from 4 to 3 o'clock.

## Racquet head open at contact

**Photo2L**                         **Photo 2M**

Many players have the tendency to hit under the ball instead of behind the ball. Naturally, what happens is you end up hitting shots that travel too high over the net and end up going long. **(Photo 2L)**

This is more likely to happen with the one-handed backhand because it's more natural to be late as opposed to the two-handed backhand and the forehand groundstrokes. The one-handed backhand is not a natural stroke for most people, so meeting the ball further out in front of your front foot can be more difficult to time. This is one of the main reasons your opponent will serve to your backhand. One handed backhand returns tend to be too high and float back for easy put-a ways. Correct this by hitting over and through the ball. **(Photo 2M)**

### Swinging full speed from 6 o'clock to 3 o'clock

Learning to have control in the speed of the racquet head will help with your consistency in keeping the ball in play in a rally. Swinging too fast, swinging too slow, and swinging late causes you to slap at the ball without control. Getting the racquet back at 6 o'clock just before the ball bounces in front of you helps you prepare early enough with a smooth and fluid motion to time the ball at contact (3 o'clock) in front of your front foot. Think of the imaginary clock that is now *on the ground and you're standing in the middle of it.* With your racquet facing the fence behind you for early preparation at 6 o'clock, your racquet head acceleration should actually start to pick up speed in the **control zone**, at 4 o'clock to make contact at 3 o'clock. If you are a righty your racquet head acceleration will pick up at 8 o'clock to make contact at 9 o'clock. When attempting to hit a winner to end the point, accelerate the racquet head with greater velocity just before you are ready to make contact with the ball in the **control zone**.

### Too late at contact

This is typically a bigger problem with the backhand, and especially the one-handed backhand. If you concentrate on where the ball is bouncing in front of you and your racquet is back quickly at 6 o'clock, you can swing forward slower and smoother to make contact at 3 o'clock. Players can sometimes get away with being a little late on the forehand groundstrokes, because their hitting arm is behind the body when properly positioned sideways to the net. On the other side of the coin, when we are set up sideways to the net to hit a one-handed backhand, our hitting arm is already positioned in front of us, which makes it more likely to be late if our timing is not just right.

## Not using your non-hitting arm to pull your racquet back

Many players underestimate the importance of their non-hitting arm. Using your non-hitting arm to pull the racquet back to 6 o'clock will help you coil and aid in turning your shoulders to generate more power to make contact at 3 o'clock.

**Photo 2N**          **Photo 2P**

Incorrect use of non-hitting arm **(Photo 2N)**.
Correct use of non-hitting arm **(Photo 2P)**.

## Not coiling enough

When you start your preparation for the one-handed backhand, use your non-hitting arm to pull the racquet back to 6 o'clock. For the two-handed backhand your shoulders will turn automatically at the same time you pull your racquet back to 6 o'clock. When you coil properly for your one-handed backhand your opponent should be able to see your back. When you uncoil it will be easier to generate more power with less effort, because you will be using your legs, hips, and shoulders through the stroke.

Photo 2Q (correct)

Photo 2R (incorrect)

**Slicing the backhand (majority of the time)**

Slicing the one-handed backhand comes naturally and is an easier way to keep the ball in play. However, if you want to raise your level and hit more offensively, learn to hit over and through the ball with the hitting surface of the racquet facing 10° closed at contact. **(Photo 2S)**

When you hit down on the ball with down force, you brush up at the same

**Photo 2S**

time to finish up and across at 11-o'clock. As counter intuitive as it may sound, you will impart topspin along with drive to keep the ball low so it penetrates like a missile. Drill yourself to hit over the ball on all of your one-handed backhands during practice regardless of how many mistakes you make. Be firm and make yourself do it.

### There are Several Good Reasons to use the Backhand Slice

1) If you're late it buys you some time to get back in position.
2) If the ball bounces too high out of your natural and comfortable hitting zone (well above your shoulders).
3) To change the pace of the ball because your opponent is getting into a good rhythm. This also works well against tall opponents. Tall players or players who have a mobility problem can not get down to the ball consistently as easily as players who are shorter that move well.

### Not hitting at the apex. Waiting for the ball to descend

It's a natural tendency to wait for the ball to come to you. When you do that, you put yourself in a defensive position by letting the ball play you. The game of tennis is about Time, Place, Angles, and Options. Hitting the ball at the apex gives you a big advantage to hit earlier and more aggressively, taking time away from your opponent getting into place. Furthermore, it will usually mean the contact point is above the net, allowing you the opportunity to hit down the ball and drive through in a straight line. The other advantage is the opportunity to impart horizontal groundstrokes. *On the imaginary clock that is positioned directly in front of you*, the path of your racquet goes from 2 o'clock across to 10 o'clock . (Opposite for righties.)

In the one-handed backhand, hitting at the apex is far more difficult since you lose power the higher the contact point. Instead, think in terms of hitting on the rise. By comparison, a two-handed backhand is like having two forehands. Your right hand is now the dominant hand, making it easier to come over the ball as opposed to a one-handed backhand.

## Waiting for the ball to come to you

By waiting for the ball to drop you have to hit up and over the net as opposed to directly hitting through the ball with the horizontal ground stroke for a more offensive and aggressive shot. When waiting for the ball to come to you, you are not only playing defensively, but more importantly giving your opponent time to get in position for the next shot. Always keep in mind that game of tennis is about Time, Place, Angles, and Options. Hitting the ball that much earlier (at the top of the bounce) takes time away from your opponent to get in place. If their mobility is poor it makes it that much easier to win the point without having to hit the ball with so much velocity. Hitting on the rise is the best, but of course it's much more difficult. I recommend learning to hit at the top of the bounce first, then trying to hit earlier by hitting on the rise. You'll discover winning a point will become much easier.

## Not having your racquet in front of you in the ready position

It's common to see tennis players with their racquets hanging down the side of their leg when waiting for a reply. This practice makes it far more difficult to time the ball at the proper contact point, especially when hitting a one-handed backhand. The practice is having the racquet in the ready position in front of your chest just below your chin, so that you look over the racquet rather than through the racquet. The best is when you hold the racquet across your body, waist high with the Continental Grip. It is far more economical for you to be prepared to hit a forehand groundstroke or a backhand groundstroke or any unexpected volleys when you are in the correct position.

**Photo 2T**

**Photo 2U**

Incorrect ready position
**(Photo 2T)**.

Correct ready position
**(Photo 2U)**.

Correct ready position, most
economical  **(Photo 2V)**

**Photo 2V**

## Weight on the wrong foot (back foot)

**Photo 2W**

Putting your weight on the back foot can result in poor balance and can be the cause of lack of power and consistency. **(Photo 2W )** Typically, leaning back prohibits you from preparing quickly enough to adjust your weight forward through the ball. Not moving to the ball will catch you off guard and off balance, and cause you to hit off the back foot. Failing to get out of the path of the ball quickly enough will cause you to be late with your foot work for transferring your weight forward. There will be times when you are forced to hit off the back foot because the ball comes back too fast and deep. When confronted with a ball that is hit deep with pace, try to resist moving away from the ball. Stand your ground and hit the ball on the rise.

## Not staying down at contact

We see the pros lifting off the ground when hitting their groundstrokes, so it's natural for us to want to emulate them. But the fact is, you are witnessing their natural momentum lifting them up due to the pace, depth, and position of the ball at the moment. Your best players are the ones not lifting off the ground as much. Once you elevate off the ground your racquet head is lifting too. When that happens it's far more difficult to have control of your shots. What you want to do is stay down through the shot and move horizontally not vertically. This gives you more control through the contact point with consistency.

## Not keeping racquet head speed consistent

A common problem is the inconsistency of racquet head speed when hitting groundstrokes. Learning to have control in the speed of the racquet head will help tremendously in keeping the ball in play in a rally. When swinging too fast or too slow, you end up slapping at the ball without control. By having your racquet in place before the ball bounces in front of you, you can prepare early enough with a smooth and fluid motion. Time the ball at 3 o'clock to make contact out in front of your front foot. Think of the imaginary clock that is now *on the ground and you're standing in the middle of it* with your racquet facing the back fence for early preparation at 6 o'clock.

Your racquet head acceleration should start to pick up speed at 4 o'clock to make contact at 3 o'clock. If you are a righty your racquet head acceleration will pick up at 8 o'clock to make contact at 9 o'clock. The key is to keep the racquet head speed as consistent as possible to stay in the rally. When attempting to hit a winner to end the point, accelerate the racquet head with greater velocity just before you are ready to make contact with the ball.

## Running around your backhand to hit a forehand

The forehand groundstroke is by far the most natural stroke in the game. The natural tendency and is to run around your backhand to hit a forehand. Learning to accept your backhand will prevent you from running around it to hit a forehand. To be as confident with your one-handed backhand as your forehand, learn to hit over the ball the majority of the time as you would with your forehand groundstroke. This concept is not easy for everyone. Many instructors will automatically instruct you to slice the backhand if you play with a one-handed backhand. Depending on your objective, slicing your one-handed backhand the majority of the time is a good concept. However, if you want to raise your level to the best of your ability, you are going to have to learn to hit over the ball on a one-handed backhand.

There are three good reasons to slice the one-handed backhand: (1) When the ball bounces too high over your hitting zone: (2) When stretched out wide and the ball gets behind you, it will buy you some time: (3) For a change of pace to give your opponent a different look. Tall players have a much more difficult time bending (especially tall two-handed backhand players) than shorter players, because hitting a good slice makes the ball stay low.

You should commit to coming over the one handed backhand if you want to play at the highest level. You wouldn't slice your forehand unless the ball got behind you and you were late, and you needed to buy your self some time. So why then should you program yourself to slice the one-handed backhand the majority of the time? Keep in mind slicing is not wrong. The only problem is the high level player is aware that hitting off of a slice offers the opportunity to take control of the point, especially a slice that floats and sits up. Remember, you must accept it in your <u>mind first</u> in order for it to translate to muscle memory to your racquet. But, this will only work well if you can be consistent enough to keep the ball in play. It requires a lot of dedication to be able to come over the ball the majority of the time on a one handed backhand. Good defense wins lots of matches.

## Miss hits

This is a common problem I see especially at the club and recreational levels. The best way to cure miss hits is to think of *that imaginary clock that is on the ground and you're standing in the middle of it.* Accelerate your racquet just before making contact with the ball from 4 o'clock to 3 o'clock and not from 6 o'clock to 3 o'clock. By having this mindset, you will have a much better chance of hitting the sweet spot as opposed to swinging full speed from 6 o'clock to 3 o'clock.

Racquet path - Elevated One-Handed Backhand ( left-handed players).

Grip of choice-Full Eastern Backhand grip, Semi-Western Backhand grip or Continental grip

Racquet path – Inverted One-Handed Backhand ( left-handed players).

Grip of choice- Full Eastern Backhand grip, Continental grip or Semi-Western grip

The Inverted One-Handed Backhand is useful for generating an excessive amount of spin, and for creating greater angles. However it is much more difficult to do as opposed to the Inverted Forehand ground stroke.

Racquet path – Horizontal One-Handed Backhand ( left-handed players).

Grip of choice - Full Eastern Backhand grip or Semi-Western Backhand grip.

## Two-Handed Backhand

As an instructor I feel that it is important for students to try both the one-handed and two-handed backhands to see which one works best for them.

The advantage of hitting a two-handed backhand is it's easier for some people to generate power. This is usually the case for most women and young children. The two-handed backhand can also be recommended to people who are suffering from some form of arm problem. It's also an advantage when returning serve on those high bouncing balls that are hit above the shoulders. Having a two-handed backhand is almost like having two forehands.

When you are returning a high bouncing service return above your shoulders, it is much easier to return it with a two-handed backhand offensively, because you are now hitting with the dominant hand (right hand). The disadvantage of a two-handed backhand is that you lose the reach that you have with a one-handed backhand and you don't have the variety of different strokes as with a one-handed backhand. History proves there have been more one-handed backhand champions with longer careers than two-handed backhand champions.

When hitting a two-handed backhand, the right hand is dominant for left-handed players (opposite for right-handed players). The grip of choice is the Continental Grip for the non-dominant hand, and the Eastern Forehand Grip for the dominant hand. Holding the Continental Grip for the non-dominant hand is recommended because it allows for a longer reach when you release your left hand for those hard-to- reach shots. Furthermore, holding the Continental Grip also gives you the option to be prepared to change from a two-handed backhand to a one-handed backhand if you so desire. The other grip option would be the Semi-Western for your right-hand and the Continental for your left hand. A Semi-Western Grip allows you to impart more spin on the ball because of the angle of the racquet on the ball. The most economical grip option would be to hold a Full Eastern Forehand Grip with both your right hand and left hand. Depending on your level of play this is usually the best option when learning the two-handed backhand for the first time.

Since your right hand is the dominant hand for a two-handed backhand, a good way to make sure you learn to hit out through the ball is to practice hitting with your right arm only. Hit a full ball hopper of balls by bouncing the ball to yourself but using your right arm only to hit the ball until you get comfortable. Then add the non-dominant arm to the racquet handle. The path of the racquet swing is relatively the same as the one-handed backhand. On *that imaginary clock standing directly in front of you*, the path of the racquet would go from 5 o'clock up and across your body to 11 o'clock and over your left shoulder as if to scratch your back. The only major difference is the full rotation of your shoulders when finishing the stroke. When you have completely uncoiled and completed the stroke, your right shoulder should be facing the net. And most importantly **freeze your head** as you watch the ball at contact.

Imagine standing in the middle of *that imaginary clock that is on the ground* with your racquet facing 6 o'clock. The path of your racquet swinging forward to make perfect contact would be at 3 o'clock. But the key to consistency is to accelerate the racquet just before making contact with the ball - about a foot before contact in the **control zone** – from 4 o'clock to 3 o'clock. The area between 6 o'clock and 4 o'clock represents the momentum of the racquet going forward.

Racquet path -Two-Handed Horizontal Backhand Ground Stroke for left-handed players.

Grip of choice (for right hand) -Full Eastern Forehand grip, Semi-Western grip or Full Western grip.

Grip of choice (for left hand) -Continental grip, Full Eastern

Forehand grip.

Racquet path –Two-Handed Elevated Backhand Ground Stroke for left-handed players.

Grip of choice (for left hand) -Continental grip or Full Eastern Forehand grip.
Grip of choice (for right hand)-Semi-Western grip, Full Eastern Forehand grip or Full Western grip.

Racquet path - Two-handed Inverted Backhand Ground Stroke for left-handed players.

Grip of choice (for left hand)-Full Eastern Forehand grip, Continental grip, Semi-Western grip or Full Western grip.

Grip of choice (for right-hand)-Full Eastern Forehand grip, Semi-Western Forehand grip, or Full Western Forehand grip.

# Overcoming Natural Tendencies

## Not freezing your head as you watch the ball at contact.

It is a normal reaction to want to look up over the net at your intended target at the same time you are making contact with the ball. **(Photo 3B)** Once you develop the muscle memory of freezing your head as you watch the ball at the point of contact, your confidence level will rise. Concentration is a major factor in order to be consistent in keeping your

**Photo 3A**

head still as you watch the ball at contact. The ball will appear as big as a baseball once you start disciplining yourself to freeze your head as if posing for a picture. **(Photo 3A )**

## Looking over the net at contact

**Photo 3B**

## Five Tips for Keeping your Head Still:

1) Look for the blur of the racquet head through the contact zone. You'll see a blur of the racquet head as it goes through the hitting zone. If you don't see the blur, you are prematurely looking over the net at the intended target. You should see the ball for the first time when it is pasting over the net or on the other side of the court.
2) After watching the ball at the point of contact, your chin should end up resting on your shoulder when your stroke is completed.
3) Concentrate on the color of the ball at the point of contact. You'll find it is much easier to track the ball on courts that are part sun and part shade.
4) Finish the stroke before looking over the net regardless of how unorthodox your stroke may be.
5) Keep your chin facing the alleys as you make contact with the ball.

## Incorrect dominant hand

For left-handed players the right hand is in control of the stroke for the two-handed backhand (Opposite for right-handed players). The left hand assists the right hand for the two-handed backhand. A good way to practice this is to hit a ball hopper of balls with your racquet using your right arm only. When you feel confident add your non-dominant hand. A good habit to get into is to change your grip on the non-dominant hand to a Continental Grip so you have the option of slicing those hard-to-reach balls. This also gives the proper grip if you decide the one-handed backhand is best for you.

# Not finishing the stroke over the opposite shoulder

**Photo 3B (incorrect)**          **Photo 3C (correct)**

A common problem is ending the stroke below the waist. Finishing up and across the opposite shoulder helps in your follow-through for a more complete finish. Keeping in mind the imaginary clock *standing directly in front of you,* left-handed players swing from 5 o'clock up and across to 11 o'clock, as if to scratch your back (7 o'clock to 1 o'clock for right-handed players).

## Not freezing your head at the point of contact when running down a ball

Freezing your head is a lot easier during a lesson when you're fed the ball comfortably in the perfect spot. But, during real play, it's much more difficult to maintain concentration. It's a natural tendency to worry about the placement or even where your opponent may be. What's important here is **where you saw your opponent last.** Think of airline pilots. They don't look out the windshield as we do driving a car ; they read their gauges. The racquet head is your gauge to read. Looking at the intended target over the net will not help as much as focusing on the ball at the contact zone.

## Racquet not back before the ball bounces

Good preparation includes having the racquet back just before the ball bounces in front of you. Keep your swing fluid and without pauses. This helps your timing and makes it easier to generate racquet head speed for power. Get your racquet back quickly to the 6 o'clock position and accelerate from 4 o'clock forward to 3 o'clock smoothly. Not only will your timing be better, but you'll find it feels good on your arm because the contact point is made out in front of you. You'll have your arm and body behind the ball instead of the ball behind your body.

## Waiting for the ball to descend

Hitting the ball at the apex gives you an edge and a big advantage to hit the ball earlier and more aggressively. Taking the ball at the top of the bounce takes time away from your opponent to get into place. Furthermore, taking the ball at the top of the bounce will usually mean the contact point is above the net which will allow you the opportunity to drive through the shot. Also, when making contact at the apex you have access to better angles and more options. The other advantage is the opportunity to impart the horizontal groundstroke, which means on the imaginary clock that is positioned *directly in front of you*, the path of your racquet will go from 2 o'clock across to 10 o'clock.

## Weight on the wrong foot (back foot)

Putting your weight on the back foot can result in poor balance and a lack of power and consistency. ( **Photo 3D)** Leaning back hampers you from preparing quickly to adjust your weight forward into the ball. Not moving to the ball catches you off guard and off balance. Not getting out of the path of the ball quickly causes you to be late with your foot work for transferring your weight forward. When confronted with a ball that is deep with pace, try to resist moving away from the ball. Stand your ground and hit the ball on the rise, and freeze your head as you watch the ball at contact.

## Jumping and lifting up when making contact on the ground stroke

**Photo 3D**

We see the pros lifting off the ground when hitting their groundstrokes so it's natural for some of us to want to emulate them. The fact is you're witnessing their natural momentum lifting them up due to the pace, depth, and position of the ball at the moment. The best players are the ones not lifting off the ground because once you elevate off the ground your racquet head is lifting. It's far more difficult to have control in your shots. You want to stay down through the shot moving horizontally not vertically for more control through the contact point with consistency. For the best results, don't try and emulate your favorite tennis star by lifting off the ground, rather stay down through the stroke for control.

## Racquet head speed varies too much

A common problem I often see is the inconsistency of the speed of the racquet head when hitting groundstrokes. Learning to have consistent racquet head accelerations will help tremendously in keeping the ball in play in a rally. Swinging too fast then swinging too slow causes you to rush and end up swinging very fast and slapping at the ball without control. Concentrating on the bounce and getting the racquet back at 6 o'clock just before the ball bounces in front of you helps you prepare early enough with a smooth and fluid motion without a hitch, so you can time the ball at 3 o'clock to make contact in front of you.

## Swinging full speed when racquet is facing back fence behind you at 6 o'clock to the contact point at 3 o'clock

Think of the imaginary clock on the ground and you're standing in the middle of it with your racquet facing the back fence for early preparation at 6 o'clock. Your racquet head acceleration should actually start to pick up speed at 4 o'clock to make contact at 3 o'clock. If you are a righty your racquet head acceleration will pick up at 8 o'clock to make contact at 9 o'clock. You are picking up racquet head speed just before making contact with the ball. The key is to keep the racquet head speed the same as close as possible to be consistent enough to stay in the rally. When attempting to hit a winner to end the point, accelerate the racquet head with greater velocity just before you are ready to make contact with the ball.

## Hitting under the ball with an open face

When you make contact with the ball too far behind the hitting zone, your racquet head ends up facing the sky resulting in hitting under the ball instead of behind the ball. This is one of the main reasons your opponent will serve to your backhand. Backhand returns tend to

be weak and float back high for easy put-aways. This is more likely to happen with the one-handed backhand because it's easier and more natural to be late as opposed to the two-handed backhand. **(Photo 3E)**

**Photo 3E**

## Hitting under the ball

One of the easiest ways to fix this problem is to think of hitting directly behind the ball with a racquet that is perpendicular to the ground or a 10° closed racquet face.

## Hitting up and across too early

When your stroke goes up and across too early, you hit into the net, wide, or inconsistently. Hit out through ball at the contact point as far as your arm can reach then go up and across your opposite shoulder as if to scratch your back. Hitting up and across requires a lot more racquet head speed to get the ball over the net. It's more important to learn to hit out rather than up and across prematurely.

## Not making contact in front of your front foot

Concentrating on where the ball bounces in front of you makes it easier to make contact in front of your front foot. You'll have your arm and body behind the ball with a laid-back wrist for better leverage. Keep in mind (it's easier to see the ball) when you're making contact in front of your body. Follow the ball off your opponent's racquet. As the ball is coming over the net, track it closely to focus on where it's going to bounce, and make contact in front of your front foot so your arm and body will be completely behind the ball. Doing this helps in stepping into the shot by getting your body weight forward for achieving more power. When your racquet is squared off you'll hit behind the ball rather than under the ball.

## Not playing the ball

Most players wait for the ball to come to them. Tennis is a game of Time, Place, Angles, and Options. Waiting for the ball to come to you will only make you end up hitting up and over the net which gives your opponent more time to get to the ball. The better choice is to hit the ball at the top of the bounce, which is usually higher than the net. This allows you to hit directly through the ball with more authority in a straight line. Instead of the ball going over the net in an arch, the ball travels over the net more aggressively in a straight line in the form of a missile with spin. Furthermore, your options are greater because you have more angles available to hit into the court. The racquet path after hitting down on the ball should finish up to 1 o'clock.

## Hitting the ball with underspin

The problem with hitting with underspin is that air rushes under the ball making it float and go long. A good way to learn control is to hit through and out on the ball at the same time you're hitting low to high. Thinking of the imaginary clock *standing directly in front of you,* the swing path of the racquet would travel from 5 o'clock up and across your body to 11 o'clock as if to scratch your back. That will stop you from chopping down on the ball and make you hit through it offensively. When your racquet head is in the position for contact, think of the top of the frame leading first with a 10° angle facing down with the bottom of the racquet head to follow. This will prevent you from hitting under the ball with an open racquet and help make contact directly through the middle of the ball driving the ball with topspin. Another good solution is to have your racquet perpendicular to the ground at contact so as to hit flat through the middle of the ball.

## Not hitting at the apex

It's a natural tendency to want to wait for the ball to come to you. But when you do that, you are letting the ball play you. You're putting yourself in the position of waiting for the ball to descend from the apex which is a major disadvantage. Hitting the ball at the apex gives you an edge and a big advantage to hit the ball earlier and more aggressively. Taking the ball at the top of the bounce takes time away from your opponent to get into place. Furthermore, taking the ball at the top of the bounce will usually mean the contact point is above the net which will allow you now the opportunity to drive through the ball. When making contact at the apex you have access to better angles and more options. The other advantage is the opportunity to impart the horizontal ground stroke, which means on that imaginary clock that is positioned *directly in front of you,* the path of your racquet will go from 2 o'clock across horizontally to 10 o'clock..

### Running around your two-handed backhand

Unlike the one-handed backhand, you have a far better chance of hitting over and through on high bouncing balls with a two handed backhand. Having a two-handed backhand is almost like having two forehands. If you're a right-handed player the dominant hand will be your left hand. If you are a lefty, it's now your right hand that is the dominant hand. When playing a two-handed backhand it's not necessary to run around your backhand. Rather continue the mindset of going to the ball to hit it at the apex and resist the temptation of running around the backhand. The two-handed backhand gives you the distinct advantage of hitting high bouncing balls outside the hitting zone with authority. If you don't hit the ball earlier on the rise with a one-handed backhand, you are forced to slice the ball if it bounces too high outside a comfortable hitting zone. The disadvantage with a two-handed backhand is you lose some reach as opposed to the one-handed backhand that allows you to get at those hard to reach shots a little easier.

### Not having your racquet back early enough when running down a backhand

It's a natural tendency to have the racquet in front of you when running down a one-handed or two-handed backhand. For the best results, your racquet should be facing the fence behind you at 6 o'clock, just before you're ready to set up to hit the ball. Once you are ready to make contact with the ball, concentrate on coming forward with your racquet to make contact at 3 o'clock. Get in place as quickly as possible so you can exchange your weight forward through the stroke. If you are late getting into place, the best you can do is run through the contact point.

## Miss hits

This is a common problem I see at most levels especially with beginners and at the club and recreational level. The best way to cure this common problem of miss hits is to think of that imaginary clock that is now *on the ground and you're standing in the middle of it.* Imagine accelerating your racquet just before making contact with the ball (on our imaginary clock that would be from 4 o'clock to 3 o'clock and not from 6 o'clock to 3 o'clock). By having this mindset, you will have a much better chance of hitting the sweet spot as opposed to swinging full speed from 6 o'clock to 3 o'clock (contact point).

## Lack power

To be able to develop power for your two-handed backhand you must have proper technique along with good timing and tremendous racquet head speed. Position your racquet close at 10° on the ball at contact swinging low to high. Make sure your contact point is made in front of your front foot so as to have your arm and body behind the ball. A tremendous amount of racquet speed is required just before contact.

# Serve

Serve is the most important stroke of all. It's the only stroke where you are totally in control. The serve gives you the opportunity to immediately go on offense while setting yourself up for good position for the next shot. In doubles, the serve is a major tool for assisting you and your partner for better positioning on the next shot to win the point. When your serve isn't working or your rhythm is off, it usually affects the rest of your game. Chances are if you are not good at serving you can end up losing the match. Fortunately, the serve is the one stroke that's easily practiced alone. Spending a lot of time practicing the serve is time well spent.

Serving well does not relate to how many mph you can produce. Placement, variety, and spin are keys to a good serve. After you've developed these key ingredients, go for pace. You may practice your form in front of a mirror to visualize your form, or against a wall or a back board to gain control. You'll know you are serving well when your first service percentage is anywhere around 65 % or more. Never lose sight of the fact that pace is not always the most important goal in serving. Placement, spin and variety will prove to pay more dividends than pace. Always watch the ball at the point of contact and freeze your head.

There are four serves available to you at any time. The grip of choice used by most tennis pros for the serve is the Continental Grip. The Continental Grip puts the racquet head at such an angle on the ball that it helps add more spin with less effort. Some players use an Eastern Backhand Grip to get even more angle on the ball for greater amount of spin. Keep in mind that almost every second serve will be either a Slice Serve or a Kick Serve. Think of those two as your "Go-To" serves.

The foundation of the serve is the **toss**. Keep it simple by having a consistent toss that is out in front you at the same height every time. This will help in having a good, reliable serve with a reasonable amount of power. The old saying is you're only as good as your second serve, no matter who you may be. If you don't have an effective second serve, it's because most of us think in terms of power first. It's the classic mistake at all levels. The great Roger Federer had an average serve at best for several years when he first came out on tour. But his placement and variety proved you didn't have to hit 130 mph serves to be dangerous.

Practice your second serve more than your first serve. Most players at the club and recreational level have a very pedestrian second serve. The reasons include lack of racquet head speed, bad timing,

 improper technique, or lack of confidence. The key to a good second serve is to maintain plenty of racquet head acceleration with a significant amount of spin. Most anyone can walk up to the base line and crush the ball. But to do it with control is a whole different story!

**Photo 4A ( kick serve)**

The Kick Serve can be hit with a ball toss positioned directly over your head – where the ball would land on your head if you did not hit it. The path of the racquet for the Kick Serve goes from 5 o'clock to 11 o'clock on the ball (**Photo 4A**). The object is to brush across the ball to cause it to bounce up high to the right of a right handed returner. The path of your toss goes from left to right while the path of your racquet goes from right to left as you pronate at contact. As the racquet collides with the ball a tremendous amount of spin is imparted, causing the ball to hit the ground in front of a right-handed returner and bounce up high above their right shoulder.

In a move known as the "American Twist," you can impart topspin by holding the Eastern Backhand Grip or the Continental Grip with a toss to the right of the right shoulder for a left-handed player (*at 1 o'clock on the imaginary clock standing directly in front of you*). This move requires more of a bending backwards with <u>your legs and not your back.</u> When executed correctly, the ball will have topspin and bounce off in the opposite direction. For right-handed returners the ball bounces up high off to their right. The safety factor is greater because of the relatively high margin of height over the net by hitting up under and over the ball.

A common problem I see over and over again with this particular serve is the improper bending at the back or waistline instead of the legs. This is especially important when learning this serve at a young age. Constantly repeating the improper technique can easily result in premature lower back problems.

## Photo 4B (slice serve)

The other serve often used to lessen the chance of making a mistake is the Slice Serve. The Slice Serve involves making contact with the ball with your racquet angled on the left side of the ball. At the same time, you square your shoulders off to the net so the ball will spin off the court and pull the returner off to their left. This motion is achieved by pronating as you make contact on the left side of the ball. It allows you to hit with more pace and less effort. It's been said that when you pronate, you can easily get 15 mph more pace.

The Flat Serve is usually a serve that is hit as a first serve, and has a lower success rate than the Slice or Kick Serve. To hit a Flat Serve successfully is to have the angle of the racquet head squared off to hit the middle of the ball. When you hit a Flat Serve you will have more pace as opposed to spin.

**Photo 4C (flat serve)**

To hit a Reverse Serve is to make contact on the inside of the ball, or the right side of the ball. When the ball hits the ground it skids off to the right side of the returner in almost the same effect as a Kick Serve but the ball stays much lower to the ground. Instead of the ball kicking up high to the right of the returner, the ball slices off lower to the right of the returner's right side. This is a serve that is hardly used these days because the margin for error is much too great.

**Photo 4D (reverse serve)**

If you are experiencing coordination or strength issues with your shoulder or arm, the Under Hand Serve is a legal and effective stroke. There's nothing embarrassing with the concept of serving under hand. I recommend the serve to some of my seniors for a variety of reasons. The motion is exactly the same as a tennis instructor incorporates to feed

**Photo 4E (underhand serve)** balls to students during a lesson.

There is little to no stress on the arm. The Under Hand Serve gives you the ability to impart spin or slice with a reasonable amount of pace so you can drive the ball as you do your groundstroke and vary the height over the net.

For example, if you want to put spin or slice on the ball, carve or shave the left side of the ball. That will make the ball spin off to your opponent's left when the ball hits the ground. To gain more height over the net, hit under the ball with your racquet facing up. For more pace it's important to accelerate the racquet just before you're ready to make contact with the ball.

The key to hitting an Under Hand Serve is to toss the ball out in front of you between the height of your waist and knees while your chest and belly are facing the net. If you toss the ball too high, finding your rhythm will be more challenging. Hold the ball with your four fingers and thumb so the ball is not resting in the palm of your hand. By doing this you lessen the chance of the ball rolling off your fingers in a rotating motion. Keep your tossing arm straight but relaxed out in front of you into the court with a slow, smooth motion starting between knee and waist level. Whichever direction the palm of your hand faces, the hitting surface of the racquet faces the same direction. Feed the ball out in front of you and hit slightly under the ball as you would when hitting your forehand groundstroke. Freeze your head as you're watching the ball at the point of contact.

## Overcoming Natural Tendencies

### Not freezing your head at contact when watching the ball

It is natural to drop your head, rush to hit the ball, or pause during the service motion. Hold the ball with your four fingers and thumb as if you are holding a coffee cup. With your tossing arm straight over your head like the Statue of Liberty, release the ball by opening your hand so the ball doesn't roll or spin off your fingers. Don't rush the toss. Think of a slow, smooth motion as if to guide the ball in place. The best place for your toss is in front of your right shoulder at 12 o'clock or just to the left of your right shoulder at 11 o'clock.

The time from when the ball leaves your hand on the toss to the time of contact determines your rhythm. If your serves are going long it's usually because your toss is too low or is too far behind your head at contact. If your serves are going into the net it could be an indication you are dropping your head when making contact with the ball or your toss is too far in front of you in the court causing you to hit down on the ball.

Lacking power in your serve indicates inadequate racquet head speed, bad timing, or improper technique. Think in terms of accelerating the racquet head just before you make contact with the ball. Be sure you are behind the ball so the weight of your body can be transferred up and out into the shot. Your toss needs to be out in front of you into the court. If your toss is too far behind your head it will be difficult to build up sufficient racquet head speed and power because your body weight will not be behind the ball.

### Not tracking the ball with the non-hitting arm

It's natural to drop your non-hitting arm prematurely. Keep your head up at contact and continue to watch the ball by Freezing Your Head. Have your tossing arm and racquet arm go up at the same time as if to say, "Hurray!" Your non-hitting arm will be up at 12 o'clock, and the dominant arm with your elbow for your left arm will be up at 9 o'clock, looking almost as if you are talking on the telephone. Not only will this help keep your non-hitting arm up longer but will also help your timing and rhythm.

### Poor ball toss

If your toss is in the wrong position, it will effect your timing. As you extend your non-hitting arm up for the toss, keep the arm straight without bending the wrist or elbow. When your arm is completely extended release the ball. If your toss is going too far in front of you, you are releasing the ball too soon. If your toss is going behind you, you're holding the ball too long. If your toss is consistently low, you are most likely releasing the ball at chest height. Think in terms of guiding the ball in place slowly and smoothly.

### Tossing motion too fast and abrupt

A common mistake is rushing the toss and making it far more difficult to lock into a rhythm. Slow everything down. Slowing your tossing motion will automatically help you relax. Slow down the tossing motion to develop consistency, rhythm, and control along with the mindset of guiding the ball in place.

### Racquet arm lagging

Once you release the ball for the toss, it's almost too late to expect your racquet to catch up and make contact in the right position. Raise both arms up together at the same time as if to say "Hurray!" and it will be easier to find your timing and maintain a comfortable rhythm without your racquet stopping.

### Not stepping forward with back foot

Remember to step forward with your back foot. When you keep your back leg back you end up swinging only with your arm instead of your whole body. Toss the ball out in front of your front foot into the court so it forces you to step into the court with your back foot to get your body weight going forward. This helps your balance and generates power with less effort. This is especially important when playing the game of doubles. You want that forward momentum for better positioning so you can take control of the net.

## Swinging full speed prematurely

If your swing goes too fast too soon, you expend too much effort to produce power. After the release of the toss, gradually pick up racquet head speed until the point of contact. Accelerate into the ball and snap your wrist just before impact as if waving good-bye and pronate.

## Poor toss

When you're in position on the baseline to serve, imagine a large clock *standing and facing directly in front of you.* In front of your right shoulder would be 12 o'clock and just to the left would be 11 o'clock (opposite for right-handed players). Tossing the ball at 12 o'clock gives you a better angle down into the court. The toss at 11 o'clock is correct, however the racquet takes a slightly longer path to the point of contact and doesn't have as good an angle down into the court as the 12 o'clock position. With the follow through of your service motion at the 12 o'clock position, it's your left shoulder that will be in line with the ball at contact for a better angle into the court. Tossing the ball at 10 o'clock forces you to swing much too far to the left with a longer path to contact. The 12 o'clock path to the ball is far more economical and direct.

When your toss continually wanders off to the left, it is an indication your tossing arm is aiming in that direction and also releasing the ball too soon, (as opposed to the tossing arm moving in the direction toward the net). If it continually goes over and behind your head you're holding the ball too long. Most importantly, your tossing arm must remain straight and relaxed from the start of the motion to the end of the motion at the time you release the ball. Breaking the wrist or bending your arm at the elbow will prevent you from tossing the ball in the correct position. For the more advanced players, having your toss moving from left to right and making contact at 12 or between 12 and 1o'clock will impart a lot of spin. On the imaginary clock *standing directly in front of you,* the toss would go across the clock from 7 to 12 or from 7 to 1. One o'clock is the position normally used with the higher level players who want to hit the kick serve.

### Front foot moving

Moving your front foot usually results in a foot fault. When your front foot moves, you automatically put yourself out of position, jeopardizing the consistency of the toss. As your tossing arm goes up, push down into the court on the balls of your feet to insure they don't move out of position. Your back foot can stay back in a wide stance that some players prefer. The other stance is the pin point stance, where the back foot moves forward next to the front foot just before contact is made.

### Not coiling

Uncoiling to begin the kinetic chain is the rotation of your chest and belly away from the net in the effort to generate power for the serve. It is like the winding up of a spring then releasing it to unwind. Even just a small amount of coiling will make a difference as opposed to swinging your racquet with just your arm.

### Non hitting arm swinging off
### to the side at contact

It's a natural tendency for the non-hitting arm to swing off to the side of your body during the follow through on the serve **(Photo 4F)**. Along with poor balance, your energy is going off to the side in the wrong direction instead of forward toward the net. With your arm

tucked into your chest area on the follow through, your forward momentum is going toward the intended target as well as keeping you balanced with a greater center of gravity. With your arm tucked into the chest area you'll experience the uncoiling motion to be
 smoother and faster, and you'll be amazed on how much easier it is to generate power **(Photo 4G).**  After tracking the ball with the non-hitting arm, don't let the non-hitting arm drop off to right side of your body (for left

**Photo 4F**

handed players). Keep your non-hitting arm tucked in toward your chest. This will help in rotating and uncoiling with greater velocity like a springboard diver for generating power forward with better balance and a good center of gravity.

### Foot  Fault

When the server takes more than one step before making contact with the ball.
When your foot touches the base line or the back court before making contact.
When part of your foot extends beyond the imaginary extension of the centermark.

**Photo 4G**

## Frequently Asked Questions

### How do I get more power in my serve?

Power comes from a combination of the proper technique, excellent timing and tremendous racquet speed. Proper technique includes pronating when making contact with the ball. That combined with a tremendous amount of racquet head speed and perfect timing will help you achieve more power in your serve. **(Photo 4H)**

**Photo 4H**

### Why do I keep double faulting?

This is usually because you are dropping your head as you make contact with the ball. When your head drops, the racquet head drops.

### How do I develop a better second serve?

Maintain a tremendous amount of racquet head speed as you would to hit a first serve, but hit with a greater amount of spin. Practice your second serve more than your first serve. This will help develop your consistency and your confidence.

### How do I learn to place my serve?

Think in terms of aiming with the palm of your hand. Whichever direction the palm of your hand faces, the hitting surface of the racquet faces the same way. For better accuracy don't look across the net at the intended target. Keep your head up and perfectly still as you make contact with the ball.

### How do I hit a slice serve?

The most effective technique is to pronate on the left side of the ball ( opposite for righties). For some club and recreational players pronating may prove too difficult. An alternative is supinating (rotation of the palm up toward the sky). As you carve around the left side of the ball your palm faces up at the end of the stroke. Try not to rotate your left shoulder around by squaring it off to the net too soon. That will cause the serve to go wide outside the service box to the right. Your toss should be consistently in the same place every time. For some, tossing the ball at 11 o'clock (just to the left of your right shoulder) works very well. For others, tossing the ball at 1 o'clock (directly in front of your left shoulder for right-handed players) seems to work best.

### What's the proper grip?

The grip of choice is the Continental. All serves can be hit with this grip; however for some the Continental may be uncomfortable. Using the Eastern Forehand grip is perfectly acceptable.

### How do I stay relaxed?

 Walk up to the baseline and go through your routine before you start your service motion, whether it consists of bouncing the ball a few times or taking a few breaths before settling into position. Slow down, especially in between 1$^{st}$ and 2$^{nd}$ serves.

### How do I keep my head up?

 Many players will hit down because they drop their head when making contact. Go up to the ball as if you are going to reach up to high five it, and snap your wrist as if saying "good- bye." Focusing on the color of the ball will also help in keeping your head up. Another good concept is to focus on the blur of the racquet through impact, or watch the ball at the point of contact and freeze your head. That will prevent you from dropping your head every time.

Keep your non-hitting arm up while tracking the ball. Once your tossing arm drops, your head drops.

## How do I serve for placement?

The very first impulse for most players is to strive for power. Most people can hit the ball hard and produce an adequate amount of pace, but not necessarily pinpoint accuracy and control. Placement is far more important than pace because you can use your serve to set yourself up for better positioning on the next shot. Learning to hit the serve with more control by hitting with different spins, speeds, and heights is more effective than trying to hit with more pace and going for quick points. The ability to move the ball around the service box at any given time with control makes you very unpredictable and dangerous.

> The service box can be broken into 3 parts: A, B, and C. A is the alley, B is the body, and C is the center. Use those spots wisely according to your opponent's strengths and weaknesses, and it will pay you a lot of rewards. Rather than trying to get cheap points by killing the ball, use placement to serve to your opponent's backhand the majority of the time. This practice gives you service returns that are often weaker and float back for an easy put away.

## How do I keep from getting too much spin in my toss?

Hold the ball with your four fingers and thumb as if holding a coffee cup. As your straight and relaxed arm is at full extension, release your fingers from the ball by simply opening your hand so there will be less chance of rotation on the ball. A ball that is perfectly still or quiet makes it easier to control at contact.

## Why do my serves go long?

Your toss may be too low. You may not have enough wrist snap. Or, your toss could be too far behind your head, resulting in hitting late with a wide open racquet face.

## Why do I serve into the net?

The #1 reason is DROPPING YOUR HEAD! Watch the ball at the point of contact and <u>Freeze Your Head</u>. When your head drops, the racquet head drops. Another factor could be in a toss that's too low which doesn't offer the chance to get under the ball as easily.

## Why do I lack power?

Power is achieved by tremendous racquet head speed, good timing, and the proper technique.

## How do I control racquet head speed?

Controlled racquet speed is easily achieved by accelerating the racquet head just before making contact. The racquet head travels at 50 mph up until the moment of contact where it accelerates to 100 mph. Making perfect contact means hitting at the apex. But the toss plays a major roll. The most effective contact point is out in front and into the court so your body weight is <u>behind the ball.</u> With your full extension up to the ball, your momentum explodes upward and forward through the ball.

## How do I improve my serving technique?

Proper technique is rotating the forearm and palm of your hand away from your body at contact (pronating). It has been said that pronating can easily add 15 mph if executed properly with good timing and tremendous racquet head speed.

## How do I gain consistency?

For starters, the toss is a major factor for consistency. Practice often for consistency on your toss. Be sure the toss is routinely in the same place every time. If your toss isn't exactly right, don't hit the ball.

You'll get accustom to hitting a bad toss and ultimately you've wasted an opportunity for a good serve or you may double fault. Make it a point to practice your second serve more than the 1st. Once you develop a reliable toss focus on accelerating your racquet head speed with spin just before contact. Finding your rhythm on the serve is the key to success. From the time you release the ball on the toss to the moment of impact will be your timing. Control your service motion by maintaining a smooth and slow stroke up until that point of building racquet head speed just before contact. To help your timing, be sure not have your racquet lagging too far down by your side after releasing the ball on the toss. Instead both arms should be up above your head at 12 o'clock and 9 o'clock on that imaginary clock that is *standing directly to the left side of you.* The tossing arm is up at 12 o'clock tracking the ball while the elbow of the racquet arm is up at 9 o'clock with a continuous motion for better timing and more power. Be sure not to drop your tossing arm too soon and try not to have a hitch once you begin the stroke.

### Where do I finish the path of the stroke on the serve?

I often see players finishing their service motion on the same side of their body as opposed to finishing down and across the opposite side of their body. Finishing the stroke down and across the opposite side of your body helps in rotating into the stroke for generating more power effectively. Also, it helps in achieving the proper balance needed to generate your weight going forward.

### How do I avoid slowing down the racquet head speed for the second serve?

This is a natural tendency because of the fear of double faulting. But in order to have a good affective second serve you must have a good reliable toss and most importantly maintain good racquet head speed and impart a great amount of spin on the ball at contact. Practicing your second serve more than your first serve is far more beneficial.

# Return of Serve

Grip of Choice - The grip of choice may vary according to your particular style and strengths. If you are particularly comfortable returning with your backhand you may favor holding the racquet with a backhand grip, which could be either the Continental or the Full Eastern (providing you are a one-handed backhand player). For those of you who are more comfortable returning with your forehand, the tendency is to hold a Continental, Full Eastern, Semi-Western or Full Western. My advice is whether you are more comfortable with the backhand or forehand, it's wise to hold the Continental to quickly change grips for a forehand or backhand return. Furthermore, high level experienced players will immediately recognize what grip you are holding, telegraphing the fact that you prefer to return with that particular stroke. Holding the Continental disguises which stroke you are most comfortable returning.

Tennis has become a much faster game because players are bigger and stronger, and technology allows them to generate power much easier. We've heard that you should have your racquet in the ready position in front of your chest just below your chin. Especially for one-handed backhand players, my advice is to have your racquet position across your body at waist height and/or slightly higher going from left to right. If you are a left-handed player your racquet head would be in front or slightly above your right hip or up just in front of the right side of your chest. Positioning your racquet across your body in front of you at waist height or just above allows you to be prepared for any backhand return or any shots that come into your body that don't allow you the time to move your feet. If you are a two-handed backhand player, keeping your racquet in front of you, just below your chin in front of your chest, is still the position of choice. You will immediately find how much more economical it is to have your racquet positioned across your body with the Continental grip as opposed to having the racquet positioned in a vertical way in front of your chest below your chin.

# Overcoming Natural Tendencies for the Return of Serve

## Not freezing your head as you watch
## the ball at contact

Keeping your head perfectly still is the best way to be consistent in returning serve. Controlling your head from moving as you watch the ball at contact is critical. Here are four ways to help you learn to <u>freeze your head</u> as you watch the ball at contact for better return of serve.

1. Look for the blur of your racquet head through the contact zone. You'll see just a trail or a blur of the racquet head as it goes through the hitting zone. If you don't see it, you are starting to look over the net at the intended target prematurely. You should see the ball for the first time just past the net after you've hit it. You should not see it on your side of the court when lifting your head to look up to see where the ball is going. This can be very difficult to master at any level, but it is the most important muscle memory any tennis player needs to learn.
2. Your chin should end up resting on your shoulder when you finish the stroke (if it is a forehand or a two-handed backhand).
3. Focus on the color of the ball. Focusing on the color makes it easier to track the ball on courts where there is a combination of sun and shade.
4. Try completely finishing your stroke first, then look up over the net.

## Not having the racquet back early enough

The common mistake is waiting much too long to prepare your racquet back to 6 o'clock. Many players wait to get their racquet back after the serve has hit the ground in front of them. Prepare your racquet before the ball bounces in front of you. Better yet, your racquet should be back at 6 o'clock before the serve reaches the net. This is especially helpful on very fast paced serves.

# Not practicing the return of serve enough

Make it a point to spend as much time or more practicing the return of serve as you would your groundstrokes. It's easy to walk out to the tennis court with a ball hopper full of balls and practice your serve or your groundstrokes. Drop one ball after another and practice your technique for groundstrokes. Hitting up against the wall or a backboard works just as well, providing you have a reasonable amount of control to keep the ball coming back to you. You'll need a practice partner or a ball machine to practice your return of serve effectively. The return of serve is one of the most important shots in the game. More players can serve well than return serve well, simply because it's easier to practice your serve alone as opposed to needing someone to serve to you.

## Standing in too close

Standing in too close forces you to have to hit the ball on the rise. Hitting the ball on the rise is good when it takes time away from your opponent to get into place. The problem is, it's one of the most difficult shots to make. My advice is to move back far enough to make contact at the top of the bounce. If you still feel that's not enough time to react to the serve, step back far enough so you can hit the ball as it descends. You want to be able to step into the ball with your body weight going forward. Once you get your timing and start to read the opponent's serve, it will be easier to move in and take the return early.

## Taking the racquet too far back on big serves

The natural tendency is to bring the racquet as far back as 6 o'clock. That causes you to rush to make solid contact at 9 o'clock. On big serves you want to use the pace to do all the work for you. A short backswing allows you a smooth and controlled forward swing. Imagine the racquet embedded in your belly with your toes pointing toward the net. Turn the top part of your body from your waist up enough to have your chest and belly facing sideways to the net. The racquet now will be facing back as far as 8 o'clock for a forehand on that imaginary clock that is on the ground that *you're standing in the middle of.*

## Not hitting out and through at contact

The natural tendency is to come up and across your body too soon, resulting in brushing across the ball instead of hitting through the ball. On the imaginary clock *you're standing on,* make contact at 9 o'clock and continue the forward motion to 10 o'clock for a forehand. That will help you from prematurely lifting your racquet up and across your body too soon. When you picture hitting through the contact zone to 10 o'clock, you extend out through the ball and the results will be a good deep return.

## Not split stepping

Standing flat-footed or on the back of your heels doesn't help you prepare to explode quickly in any given direction or get your weight moving forward to the ball. As your opponent is ready to make contact with the ball you should be landing on the balls of your feet with your legs shoulder width apart and your body weight leaning forward. This will help you explode in any direction needed to get to the ball as quickly as possible. Split step just as your opponent is getting ready to make contact and you will be surprised how much easier it is to get in position.

## Waiting for the ball

It's a normal reaction to wait for the serve to come to you and descend. You want to step in and across to get to the ball early and cut off the path of the incoming ball. Instead of moving off to the right or left, move in and across to the right or left getting to the return earlier. Concentrate on where the ball bounces in front of you so you can step into the ball and make contact at the top of the bounce or, better yet, on the rise. Think of the imaginary clock *that is on the ground and you're standing directly in the middle of it.* If you're moving across to the left on the return you would be moving to 9 o'clock for the forehand or moving to the right would be 3 o'clock for the backhand. But if you're moving in and across to cut off the path of the ball, you are now moving to 10 o'clock to hit a forehand return and 2 o'clock to hit a backhand return. Remember to <u>freeze your head</u> as you watch the ball at contact.

## Not concentrating on the ball on the toss of your opponents racquet head

Standing and waiting to return serve with your feet shoulder width apart on the balls of your feet with your racquet in front of you is the perfect ready position. However, your focus should be on the ball coming off your opponent's racquet head. For the much higher level players, reading the toss is crucial. Knowing and understanding your opponent's toss will prepare you for responding to a particular serve. Knowing and understanding what to look for in the toss will help your anticipation and judgment of where your opponent is planning to place the serve. Higher level players will also take notice when their opponent is tossing the ball slightly to the right of their right shoulder which means that the server is going to hit a Kick Serve. When the server tosses the ball directly in front and in line of their right shoulder it usually means they're going to hit a Flat Serve. When the server tosses the ball just to the left of their right shoulder it usually means they are going to slice the serve. The best servers will not telegraph what kind of serve they are going to hit because they have the ability to toss the ball in the same place most of the time.

# Volleys

## Full Volleys, Swing Volleys, and Half Volley

Grip of choice- The Continental, Eastern Forehand and the Eastern Backhand (for the backhand volley).

The volley is a typical stroke that is hit before the ball bounces. It is also used to help prevent you from playing defensively and allows you to go on offense. The volley can be an advantage when used on a particular court such as grass or clay that may present a bad bounce. One of the many advantages to the volley is giving you the opportunity to get closer to the net for a better position and a wider choice of angles. You can volley from anywhere on the court. Most people are under the impression that you should only volley when you are close to the net. But you can also volley from no man's land (in between the baseline and the service box line) if you feel instinctively it helps you to get in better position.

During many matches you see players battle it out from the baseline. Sometimes these players are called "counter punchers." Counter punchers are players that are usually very consistent and wait patiently for the perfect opportunity to go for an outright winner. Unfortunately, most counter punchers are uncomfortable when it comes to having to volley. The joke is they are allergic to the net. Learning to volley gives you the opportunity to have an all around game so you don't become a one-dimensional player. Even if you prefer to play the game from the baseline, knowing how to volley gives you that extra edge to win the point when you are presented with a short ball and your approach shot is returned, forcing you to volley. There have been great tennis players that could not volley but still became champions. However there have been more great champions who volley extremely well. In the game of singles you have a choice in how much you want to incorporate the volley in your game. Learning to volley is a must when playing the game of doubles at any level.

One of the most common problems is waiting for the ball to come to you. When you wait for the ball to come to you, you are not using your legs. Move to the ball as it comes over the net. By doing this you are incorporating your legs into the volley. As you step into the volley think about intercepting the ball so you make contact further out in front of you. Otherwise, the ball gets too close to you and you don't have the leverage needed to generate power. Almost everyone will have the natural tendency to chop down and slap at the ball with a loose wrist at contact, resulting in volleys going into the net, long, or losing control all together. Another common mistake is stopping suddenly when making contact with the ball. Once you make a sudden stop your head will drop. When your head drops, your racquet head drops and a big arrow of energy goes straight down into the court instead of staying level and going forward toward the intended target. When it comes to volleys, players will make the mistake of doing more than they need to do, such as taking their racquet too far back behind their head. A good way to correct this is to stand facing the net looking straight ahead at the fence behind the baseline. With your racquet in position in front of you, bring your

**Photo 5A**

racquet back until you can no longer see the racquet in your peripheral vision. At that point you've taken the racquet too far back. You should always be able to see the racquet in front of you unless you are hitting a swing volley. As the ball comes over the net, extend the hitting arm to intercept the ball. You'll see that your elbow is not jammed into your side but is extended out away from your body and toward the net. You don't want your arm fully extended to the point where it is completely straight and stiff. However, you want your arm extended to the point where it will allow you some forward momentum in the way of a punch when making contact **(Photo 5A).**   Supinate as you make contact behind the ball. When done correctly the palm of your hand rotates upward so that your racquet face is toward the sky at the end of the volley. Hitting under the ball is a natural tendency but will result in your volleys popping up. Try to think of keeping your racquet parallel to the height of the ball you want to volley. This will make it easier to hit the back of the ball as you supinate rather than hitting under the ball. If the volley is below the top of the net, you are forced to hit up under the ball but stay down by bending at the knees and not the waist, and don't lift up when making contact with the ball. Think of that imaginary clock *that is standing directly to the* left *of you,*, or *to the right of you* (for right-handeds) players). The path of your racquet for the volley for left-handed players goes from 9 o'clock across to 3 o'clock; for righties from 3 o'clock to 9 o'clock. Resist from pulling the racquet across and down your body too soon. This will also help you volley horizontally towards the intended target. Most importantly have firm but relaxed wrists. If your wrist is not firm enough at contact you will not have the control needed to hit a solid volley.

### The Swing Volley

A swing volley is just like a ground stroke but the ball doesn't touch the ground. It is to your advantage when hitting a swing volley not let the ball descend. Making contact at shoulder height will make it easier for you to hit through the stroke horizontally to be more aggressive. Be sure not to end the stroke down below your waist. If the imaginary clock *were standing directly in front of you,* making contact at shoulder height would be at 10 o'clock. The path of the racquet would go from 10 o'clock across to 2 o'clock. The stroke would be horizontal, keeping the racquet path level to the ball. End the racquet path horizontally and not below the top of the net or below your waist when you make contact well above the net. If you have time to set up and plant your feet, it will be easier to balance yourself. If you feel you're late, then make contact with the ball while moving forward toward the intended target. Stay fluid and avoid stopping suddenly to keep your head and racquet head level and balanced with your body weight going forward.

The grip of choice for the swing volley is the Eastern, Semi-Western, or Full Western Forehand. Some players use the Continental, which could make it more difficult keeping the ball in the court. The angle of the racquet on the ball with the Continental would be slightly open facing the sky. Most importantly, freeze your head as you watch the ball at contact.

## Half Volley

The half volley is the only volley that touches the ground first. The half volley is like the dropkick in football. As the ball touches the ground your racquet quickly makes contact on the rise. The key to the half volley is to bend at the knees not at the waist. Stay down but freeze your head at contact. You'll have more control in the stroke. Once you lift up your racquet head lifts up with you. Since the half volley requires you to bend down low to the ball, you will be in the position of having to hit up. The best place to hit a half volley is crosscourt over the lowest part of the net so you'll have a smaller margin for error. Keep the racquet head in front of you at all times.

The grip of choice is the Continental. No grip change is required from a forehand half volley to a backhand half volley. If holding the Continental grip is uncomfortable for the forehand volley and you feel the need to change to your ground stroke grip (the Eastern forehand or the Semi-Western), by all means do so. If you find holding the continental grip uncomfortable on all your volleys in general and you find it easier to use your forehand grip for your forehand volley and your backhand grip for your backhand volley, by all means do so. Understand that playing high level tennis this would not be recommended. You just don't have the time to change grips because the exchange happens much too fast, especially at the highest level of doubles. Keep in mind changing grips is not unusual at the club and recreational level. What's important is what works best for you.

## Overcoming Natural Tendencies

## Full Volleys, Half Volleys, Swing Volleys for Forehand / Backhand

### Not freezing head when watching ball at contact

Your main objective is to keep your head very still as if you're posing for a picture as you watch the ball at contact. The volley exchange can happen so fast that you might not always have the time to follow the ball into your racquet. Concentrate on the ball coming off your opponent's racquet and focus on following the

**Photo 5B (not watching ball)** ball into your strings. Focusing on the color of the ball has also helped many of my students. Developing this muscle memory will help your consistency level dramatically.

### Looking over the net at contact

It's natural to look over the net at the intended target when making contact with the ball not only at the club and recreational level, but also at the pro level. This is one of the biggest reasons for poorly executed volleys. You'll be more consistent by freezing your head as you watch the ball at contact. That will help to prevent you from looking over the net prematurely at the intended target. This alone will build confidence at the same time help you relax. When you are confident, you are relaxed, and when you are relaxed you are usually confident **(Photo 5B)**.

## Improper grip

Executing the backhand volley with the wrong grip will prevent you from having the leverage that's needed, and can easily cause arm problems. The Continental is the grip of choice for the pros simply because the exchange at the net happens so fast it doesn't allow time for you to change grips from a forehand grip to a backhand grip. For most players the Continental is easier to hit a backhand volley than a forehand volley. Your wrist doesn't lay back as comfortably to hit a forehand volley as with the backhand volley. For most club and recreational players changing grips from the forehand to the backhand seems to be the only way possible to hit volleys. If you're a two-handed backhanded player it's best to sometimes hit a backhand volley with two hands. This is when it's especially good to learn to change grips to the Continental with the left hand when learning a two-handed backhand. When you volley with one hand it will feel natural which also helps with those hard to reach balls.

## Stepping with the wrong foot

Stepping with the wrong foot for a forehand volley with the left leg not only limits your reach but more importantly your balance and energy going forward through the ball **(Photo 1C)**. Stepping across and forward with the right leg for a forehand volley allows you better center of gravity and power through the stroke. For the backhand volley you should be stepping across and forward to the right with your left leg

**Photo 1C (not looking at ball)**

and across and forward to the left with your right leg for a forehand volley. Your center of gravity and balance will feel more secure as opposed to stepping with your left leg for forehand volley and your right leg for a backhand volley. Not stepping forward into the ball when possible is a mistake. Using our legs to volley is a must to get the most out of the stroke and to achieve a more penetrating and powerful shot.

### Not moving through the volley

I've seen players suddenly stop when making contact to volley. When you do this your energy goes down into the court rather than forward in the direction of the intended target. It's as if there's a big arrow of energy going straight down into the court rather than a big arrow of energy going straight forward in the direction of the target. When you stop suddenly your head drops down causing your racquet head to drop. Think of a car going down the road. When the car comes to an unexpected stop the front end goes down and the back end goes up. This is exactly what happens when we quickly stop to volley. Your head drops down along with your racquet head. Your head and your racquet head will remain level through the shot by not stopping. Moving through the volley means a step or two, it doesn't mean running through the shot unless your momentum demands it.

### Taking too big a swing

Beginners and some recreational players get nervous when asked to return a ball without it touching the ground first. The natural tendency for beginners is to take a big swing at the ball. To put up the racquet and block the shot seems completely unnatural. Many of my students that have been playing for years need to learn how to block a shot rather than taking too big of a swing. A good way to learn is thinking in terms of simply putting up the racquet and letting the ball bounce off it. What you're doing is simply putting up a barrier so the pace of the ball does all the work for you. Most people have a difficult time doing only that. Learning to block the volley makes for an easier put away when confronted with pace from your opponent, and allows you to expend little energy with better results. Learn to put your racquet up and block with a firm wrist with the racquet out in front of you. Most importantly, freezing your head at contact as you watch the ball will give you a clean, crisp, solid volley along with a lot of confidence.

## Taking racquet too far back behind your head

This is one of the biggest reasons volleys are difficult for most people. Taking the racquet too far back can be the cause for a late hit. When executed correctly, the contact point should be well out in front of your body. Hold a racquet in front of you in the ready position and keep looking straight ahead at the fence on the other side of the net. Looking forward, bring your racquet back slowly until you can no longer see it. It's at this point that you shouldn't go back any further. Further back will make it more difficult for you to make contact in front of you. When you volley the racquet should always be out in front of your body where you can see it, unless you're prepared to hit a swing volley which is a different story. Given the time, a swing volley is a very aggressive point ending stroke, but only if you recognize that the ball is coming slowly enough to allow you time to hit one. The best way to attack a swing volley is to go to the ball and meet it shoulder height  You'll make contact higher than the net which allows you to hit horizontally from 10 o'clock across to 2 o'clock  aggressively. Your racquet will be parallel to the ball which makes it easier to drive the shot.

## Chopping down on the ball

The natural tendency at contact is for the racquet head to drop down because of a loose wrist. It's more like slapping at the ball. When you make this mistake you carve down on the backside of the ball instead of hitting solidly through it. At contact you need to secure and firm up your wrists. Don't let the racquet drop down or slide up in an upward motion or twist in your hand. To prevent the racquet from slipping or moving in your hand, it's the baby finger, ring finger, and middle finger that should be holding the racquet the tightest. Most people make the mistake of squeezing tighter on the racquet handle with the thumb, index finger, and middle finger. When confronted with a ball that has a lot of pace, keep the racquet head completely still at contact and don't allow the racquet to move from that position. By doing this you use your opponent's pace and you'll have more control in successfully placing the volley where you intended it to go. With volleys less is more. Most importantly, freeze your head as you watch the ball and make sure the contact point is well out in front of your front foot.

### Finishing the stroke below your waist

This will cause you to severely chop down on the volley and jeopardize control of the shot by making you carve down on the backside of the ball and lose control of the shot. The end result is most likely you will hit the ball into the net or pop the ball up for an easy put away for your opponent. You'll have very little chance of hitting through the ball towards the intended target. To fix this problem imagine bringing your racquet level with the height of the ball you want to volley. Or you can think of it as keeping your racquet parallel with the height of the ball you want to volley. As you hit the volley keep the racquet on the same plane so that the path of the stroke doesn't end down below your waist. You can imagine having a table in front of you so if you finish too far down you'll hit the table. Think of that imaginary clock *positioned right next to you on your left side*. The path of the racquet for the volley would go from 9 o'clock across to 3 o'clock for left-handed players or 3 o'clock across to 9 o'clock for right-handed players. Your volleys will drive and stay low as you supinate. It's always good when you force your opponent to hit up. They will be forced to hit a defensive volley by hitting up. They can't do as much damage when having to hit up and over the net.

## Swinging across your body prematurely

It's a natural tendency to pull the racquet across your body too soon on volleys. When you do this you are no longer hitting directly through the ball. Your energy in the stroke is going across your body instead of straight ahead in the direction of the intended target. What's needed is to hit through the contact zone by keeping the racquet parallel with the ball in the direction you want to place your shot. At times the momentum will automatically carry the racquet across your body. But, that should happen on your own terms. Resist swinging across your body prematurely. Keep the racquet path going straight in the direction of the intended target and don't give in to the temptation for the racquet to finish across your body too soon. This requires concentration and muscle memory. Most importantly, freeze your head at contact as you watch the ball.

## Volley with the forehand more than the backhand

Your left arm (the racquet arm) can bend only so far for the forehand volley until your elbow is jammed into your side, unless you move to the right quickly enough to have a chance for a forehand volley. Realistically, you usually don't have that kind of time and you're almost guaranteed to be late. If the ball is moving slowly enough for you to move to the right and you can get out of the way of the ball, by all means use your forehand volley. Rely on the backhand volley the majority of the time holding the Continental grip. Your arm will be in a better position by laying across the front of your body from left to right. If you are a left-handed player and the ball quickly comes into your left hip, lift your elbow up so it's pointing up at 11 o'clock on that imaginary clock *that is standing directly in front of you.* Hit a backhand volley without ever having to move your feet or to get out of the way of the incoming ball. (For righties it's your right elbow that would lift up to 1 o'clock). By holding the Continental grip with the racquet lying across the front of your body you are prepared for any shot into your left hip, right hip, and belly without being forced to move out of the way of the path of the ball.

We've all been told to have the racquet positioned up in front of our chest just below our chin in the ready position, but technology has allowed us to hit with more power and less effort. You'll find it far more economical to have the racquet laying across the front of your body holding the Continental grip from left to right for left handed players (your racquet head would be positioned in front of your right hip or just above) and right to left for righties. If you are a two-handed backhand player I would still recommend that your preparation be vertical with your racquet in front of your chest just below your chin. Rely on hitting a backhand volley first. If you see the ball is far enough to your left, step in and across with your right foot to hit a forehand volley. If you see the ball is hit far to the right, step in and across with your left foot to hit a backhand volley.

## Hitting with an open racquet by making contact under the ball

It is a natural reaction when a player is getting ready to volley to hit under the ball. When you do this you are making contact with what is known as an open racquet face. The racquet head is slanted up under the ball facing the sky. That's okay if you have to make contact from below the top of the net. But your objective should be to get to the ball before it descends so you can hit solidly and aggressively behind and through the back of the ball. Imagine the handle of your racquet is a door knob and you are turning it clockwise. Your racquet face should end up facing the sky at the end of the stroke when you do it correctly. This is supination. This will drive your volley with authority and at the same time keep the ball low with underspin. Now that you've hit the volley with pace and underspin to keep the ball low, it forces your opponent to hit up. There's now a better chance for your opponent to be forced to hit a weak and floating defensive shot. When playing against a tall opponent, keeping the ball low works especially well. Tall people can't continually bend on a consistent basis as easily as shorter players who are closer to the ground. If you can keep your volleys low it's likely the return will be high enough over the net so you can attack the ball at the apex and easily put the volley away a winner. As long as you maintain the mindset of always being ready to go to the ball, you'll find yourself in an offensive position by hitting the volley at the apex, which in most cases will be higher than the net. Remember to freeze your head at contact as you watch the ball.

### Too close to the ball on high volleys

The obvious problem is crowding the ball. You're restricting yourself from transferring your weight forward towards the target. When the ball is higher than your shoulder move away to the right or left (depending if you're right-handed or left-handed), to give yourself distance to the ball on either a high backhand or forehand volley. This will help your balance and make it possible to transfer your weight forward. For low volleys you want the racquet to be closer to you. By positioning yourself closer to the ball you'll have better balance and center of gravity. If you bend for a very low volley and you stretch out wide in either direction, it's difficult to maintain a good center of gravity and balance. What works very well is to think of the letter "V." On top of the "V" you position yourself further away from the ball which gives you the balance needed to get your momentum moving forward without crowding yourself. The lower down you go on the "V" position yourself closer to the ball.

### Swinging, slapping and chopping down on high volleys

Once the racquet gets higher than your shoulders it's a natural tendency to want to finish in a downward motion. The problem I often see is that the downward motion is too exaggerated. You end up slapping and chopping down through the stroke well below your waist. Try to resist finishing below your waist. Finish the high volley slightly below your chest. <u>Less is always more</u>. The pace of the ball coming to you will determine how far back you should bring your racquet. If the ball is coming to you slowly, it allows you to take a bigger backswing. For the high volley keep the racquet in front of you so it doesn't cause you to be late for making contact in front of your front foot. Hitting out enables your volleys to project with authority and more pace, putting fewer balls into the net.

## Waiting for the ball to come to you

A normal reaction is to wait for the ball to descend or wait for the ball to come to you. Waiting allows the ball to play you instead of you hitting the ball at the apex. By hitting at the apex you have the advantage to volley more aggressively through the ball rather than having to hit up and over the net. You've also taken time away from your opponent to get in place. With contact well above the net you'll have better angles available and more options to place your shot.

## Not bending at the knees for low volleys

When the ball comes to you fast and low, the natural tendency is to react by bending at the waist and lowering your racquet to hit the ball. When you bend at the waist instead of your knees you don't have the balance and control needed for low volleys and forward momentum. Bending at the waist makes it a lot easier to lift up through the shot when you should be staying down. On those hard-to-get-to low volleys stay down as if you're sitting in a chair leaning with your right shoulder higher than the left shoulder and bend at the knees. Resist the temptation to lift up when making contact. Most importantly keep looking down at the ball and freeze your head.

## Contact not far enough in front of body

This is a natural tendency because it's part of the normal reaction of waiting for the ball to come to you. By not going to the ball it's easier to get caught hitting the volley too far behind you or too close to your body. The contact point should be well out in front of you where your arm is extended out in the direction you want the ball to go. This way you have your whole arm and body behind the ball but not so far extended so that your arm is completely stretched out. Maintain enough forward motion to punch through the ball. Freeze your head as you watch the ball at contact.

## Racquet brushing up or down at contact

It's a natural tendency from beginners to the pro level to brush up the backside of the ball at contact to volley. This upward motion is a reaction I see every day. Brushing up the backside of the ball prevents you from hitting through the volley because you're getting only a piece of the backside instead of a solid hit through the center. Keep the racquet head still with a firm wrist at contact and on the same level through the contact zone. This prevents you from brushing up, shaving up, or even chopping down on the ball.

## Not moving to the ball

When a car comes to an abrupt stop, the front end goes down and the back end goes up. This is essentially what happens when you go to volley and stop suddenly. Your head drops and your racquet head drops. Imagine a big arrow of energy going down in to the court rather than forward in the direction of the target. If you don't stop, the momentum of your body weight will help you go forward behind the shot in the direction of your target. When you continue to move forward through the volley your head and your racquet head stay level for more control and penetrating volleys.

## Not finishing the racquet path of the volley in the direction of the target

This will cause you to hit across the ball prematurely rather than solidly through the contact point. It also causes you to finish the stroke by quickly rushing the path of the racquet across your body. You'll lack penetration, depth, and pace. Think of the imaginary clock *standing up right next to you <u>on your left</u> side* facing north to south. With this clock facing you on your left side, imagine your forehand volley will go from 9 o'clock to 3 o'clock (for left-handed players), or 3 o'clock to 9 o'clock (for right-handed players). Your racquet will be at the same level horizontally in the direction you want to aim the volley. Think of having the racquet parallel to the ball - on the same plane as the ball you want to volley. This will ensure you'll extend and hit through the backside of the ball for more control and penetration.

## Not supinating at contact

When you fail to supinate, the ball sits up at a higher point, making it easier for your opponent to hit a driving ground stroke for an easy put away.

## Overcoming Natural Tendencies
## Half Volley
## Not freezing head at contact

Freezing your head at contact as you watch the ball <u>is and should be</u> one of your biggest objectives. Keeping your head completely still during contact as you watch the ball is a major key to being successful in hitting a good half volley. The volley can happen so fast that it's very easy to quickly pull your head up during contact. Follow the ball into your strings and focus on the color of the ball during contact. The half volley requires you to look down as if you picked a spot on the ground. When you focus on the color of the ball, continue to look down through the hitting zone right to the ground. This is a great way to keep your head and chin down to help you resist looking up. Once your head lifts, your racquet head will follow. Make it a habit to constantly remind yourself that your head and your racquet are attached. Now that your full concentration is on freezing your head at contact as you watch the ball, you should bend at the legs not the waist. Stay down through the half volley (as if you're sitting in a chair) without pulling up with your body. For better control use your arm only as you stay down through the completion of the stroke.

### Looking over the net at contact

It's also a natural tendency to look over the net at the intended target as you make contact with the ball when hitting a half volley **(Photo 6A)**. When you freeze your head as you watch the ball, you'll have your profile to the net when your racquet is making contact with the ball. When you do it correctly your chin will be tucked in by your left shoulder. Right schoulder

**Photo 6A**

for right-handed players. When the half volley is complete you should see your shot just over the net when you lift your head. Looking for the blur of the racquet at contact or focusing on the color of the ball works very well, especially on courts that have a combination of shade and sun. For strategic reasons whenever you hit a half volley it's best to go crosscourt over the lowest part of the net most of the time.

### Stepping forward with the wrong foot and not looking at the ball

Stepping with the left leg instead of the right leg limits your reach and more importantly your weight going forward through the shot with the proper balance and center of gravity. **(Photo 6B)**. Stepping across with the correct leg (the right leg) for a forehand half volley, allows proper balance and control towards the intended target. For the backhand half volley be sure to step across and forward towards the net with your left leg. Not stepping forward into the ball when possible will jeopardize your balance and forward momentum. Play the ball - don't wait for the ball to come to you. Think of intercepting the ball. That kind of thinking will keep you playing aggressively with your

**Photo 6B**

weight and momentum going forward as much as possible. Some players find it helpful to listen to the bounce and then the hit. Most importantly freeze your head as you make contact with the ball.

### Taking racquet too far back behind your body

When you attempt a half volley your racquet preparation should be very abbreviated. Taking the racquet back too far behind your body is one of the biggest reasons for poor timing or losing control of the stroke. You end up rushing the racquet back just to rush forward to catch up with the ball. Ultimately, you end up slapping at the ball, looking up over the net in a state of panic, and lifting up all at the same time. To control this stroke, keep the racquet in front of you where you can see it at all times. Contact should be made well in front of you on the half volley as on the full volley.

## Swinging across your body

Just as with the full volley (when the ball doesn't touch the ground first) resist swinging across your body too prematurely with your half volley. When you do this you're forcing yourself to brush across the ball first instead of hitting behind and through it. You want is to hit through the ball with a forward motion going in the direction of the intended target. Stay down through the shot and try not to lift up with your legs for more control until the stroke is finished. When you lift up, your racquet head will lift up resulting in brushing up the backside of the ball instead of brushing up and hitting out through the ball at the same time. The end result is likely for the ball to go into the net. Remember, as you watch the ball at contact, freeze your head and stay down through the end of the stroke.

## Too far away from the ball

This causes you to lose your balance and center of gravity in order to have control of the shot. Worse yet, you restrict yourself from transferring your weight toward the intended target. If you're bending for a half volley and stretched out wide in either direction it's nearly impossible to maintain any kind of balance and center of gravity. You'll have the obvious feeling of wanting to fall over. Position yourself closer to the ball to make it easier to exchange your weight forward. Stay down through the half volley until you finish the stroke.

## Wrist not firm at contact

When the ball is coming fast and low at your shoestrings it's a natural tendency to lift your head as you make contact with the ball and to slap at the ball because you feel rushed. Slapping at the ball will only make you lose control of the shot. The next worst possible mistake is slapping and lifting up all at the same time. The absolute last thing you want to do is slap, lift, and <u>not</u> freeze your head as you watch the ball at contact. Keep the racquet in front of you during contact, bend at the knees (not your waist) and stay down during contact with a firm wrist. Most of all keep your head down. Tell yourself to keep looking down as if picking a spot on the ground as you watch the ball at contact.

### Bending at the waist

Bending at the waist will not give you the proper balance needed to hit a dependable half volley. Bending at the knees will not only give you better balance but will bring you down closer to the ball. One very good way to get you to bend your knees is to imagine yourself sitting down in a chair. Once you're in that chair stay there until the stroke is complete. Try to resist lifting up too soon. If you start lifting up out of the chair your racquet will be sure to follow.

### Contact point too far back

Our natural tendency is to wait for the ball to come to us. Going to the ball will help make it easier to make contact in front of your right foot or left foot (for right-handed players). Concentrate on the bounce. If you focus where the ball is bouncing in front of you you'll make it easier to time the contact point in front of your front foot. Even when the ball is coming so fast and deep you can't help for the ball to get behind you, freeze your head as you watch the ball at contact. Nine times out of ten your chances of getting the ball back in play will be greater.

### Not moving through the half volley

When you stop as you're getting ready to hit, whatever body weight you have is channeled down into the court instead of going forward toward the intended target. At contact you need to keep moving slowly through the half volley so your body weight is going forward and your head stays level. Stopping suddenly during the half volley causes your head to drop down. Not lifting up as you make contact will keep your head level and the racquet head level. Don't run through but get to the ball as quickly as you can to hit it on the rise with the racquet out in front of you with a firm wrist. Move forward through the shot. Not only will you get the ball over the net, you'll have more control with your half volleys than you ever had before. Also keep in mind for strategic reasons it's best to go crosscourt over the lowest part of the net most of the time.

### FAQs

1) **My volleys keep popping up in the air and going long.** This usually happens because the racquet angle at contact is under the ball. Hit directly and squarely behind the ball when making contact.
2) **I have no power in my volleys.** Keep your wrists firm and make contact well in front of your body. Accelerate the racquet and supinate just before you're ready to make contact.
3) **My volleys keep going out.** Many players take their racquet too far back behind their head. Not only does this cause you to be late but it makes it more difficult to control the volley. If you recognize that the ball is coming slowly enough to allow you to take a full swing at the ball (a swing volley) that's okay, that is a natural tendency. But, you need to learn to keep your racquet in front of you at all times so it's visible by taking a very short backswing and have your forward motion moving in the direction of the target. On very fast-paced shots all that is needed is to keep the racquet firm and still and let the ball bounce off. Resist punching or poking at the ball. With volleys- less is more.
4) **My volleys keep going into the net.** This is because at contact

your wrist is not firm enough. Your wrist is dropping down or finishing up causing you to brush up or down the backside of the ball instead of hitting out through the middle of the ball in the direction of the target. You could be slapping or chopping down at the ball. Keep a firm wrist at contact well out in front of your body. Another common problem is suddenly stopping when making contact with the ball. Keep moving through the volley slowly, not on the run. This way your head and your racquet head will stay level with all your forward momentum going towards the target.

# Specialty Shots

## Drop Shot

**Problem**.................. Not Knowing How to Hit a Drop Shot.
**Natural Tendency**.. Too Big Of a Swing.
**The Result**.............. Ball Pops Up Too High and Floats or Drives
Like a Ground stroke.

**The Cure**................. For starters the grip of choice is the Continental grip. Using the Eastern forehand grip will work just as well for those of you who find the Continental grip uncomfortable or confusing. Think of the path of the drop shot as the letter "J". As you're preparing to make contact with the ball be sure your racket head is slightly higher than the ball. Brush down behind and under the ball as if the path of the stroke resembles the making of the letter "J." That's what's called supinating. Supinating is the rotation of the palm of your hand up towards the sky. When you supinate, the end of the path of the drop shot should have the hitting surface of the racket facing the sky. As you're making contact with the ball be sure you keep moving forward slowly through the shot so all your energy from your body weight is going towards the intended target. Be sure not to run full speed as you're making contact with the ball but move forward slowly and do not come to a sudden stop. It would be like imagining a big arrow of energy going down into the court when you come to a sudden stop. Rather you want that big arrow of energy going forward to the net towards intended target Whatever body weight you posses will help in getting the ball over the net with less effort. Most importantly watch the ball at the point of contact by FREEZING YOUR HEAD! Try to resist the natural tendency of looking over the net at the intended target when making contact with the ball. Once your head moves your racket head also moves: they are attached in a strange way.

Another easy concept of hitting a drop shot is to abruptly brush down on the backside of the ball as if you're chopping down a tree. If you find the ball is popping up too high where it is floating, then your racket face is open too much at contact. The face of the racket head is facing up under the ball pointing to the sky. Simply keep the racket head straight up and down or slightly open behind the ball in somewhat of a vertical position. Remember the natural tendency when attempting to hit a drop shot is to take too big of a back swing resulting in driving through the ball as you would on a ground stroke. Another natural tendecncy is to hit with a racket face that is under the ball facing the sky resulting in the ball floating and hanging in the air too long.

## FAQ's

1) **Which grip do I use to hit a drop shot?** - The grip of choice is the Continental grip. But if that's uncomfortable and difficult to adjust to the Eastern forehand grip that's used for the forehand groundstrokes is perfectly acceptable.

2) **When and where do I use a drop shot?** -Typically a drop shot is used when you are inside the pressuring zone (between the baseline and the service box line, also known as no man's land) and the point ending zone (service box) when your opponent is back behind or near the baseline. However, the drop shot can be used anywhere from the inside the service box and as far back as the baseline as long as your opponent is back far enough behind or near the baseline. (*A good tip to remember: whenever you drop shot or hit a half volley, it is wise to go cross court over the lowest part of the net (that's 3 feet in height), most of the time.*)

## Overcoming Natural Tendencies
## For the Drop Shot
## Not freezing head when making contact with the ball

The same as with all the strokes in the game, the most important fact and the mother of all foundations is making sure your head stays perfectly still when making contact with the ball. (This will help in being consistent.)

## Not staying sideways through the duration of the drop shot

A typical natural tendency is to bring your left shoulder around by squaring off your shoulders to the net too soon to see where you want to hit the drop shot. Instead stay sideways to the net until the racket path of the drop shot is complete. This will prevent you from hitting the ball wide out of bounds. When confronted with a situation of not being in proper position next to the ball, still execute the path of the stroke like the letter "J".Brush down and under the ball.

## Taking too big of a backswing

Bring your racket only as far back as your head so that the racket is always visible. This will prevent you from being late.

## Suddenly stopping

This will cause all your energy from your body weight going down into the court. Rather than just coming to a sudden stop keep moving forward <u>slowly</u> in the direction of the intended target. This will prevent you from hitting the ball into the net.

## Too much racket head acceleration

This stroke requires the mechanics to be slower in motion with more of a soft touch. This will help you to have more control in the stroke.

## Attempting to drop shot over the highest part of the net

When attempting to drop shot it's always wise to go crosscourt over the lowest part of the net, most of the time. This will help prevent you from hitting into the net.

## Drop shot when opponent is in good position (service box)

The biggest mistake I see day in and day out are players attempting the drop shot when their opponent is in the service box (point ending zone). The time to drop shot is when your opponent is in no man's land (pressuring zone) or better yet behind the baseline (rally zone). At this point it's wise to drop shot because you have more court available to hit into and now you're forcing your opponent to uncomfortably chase down the ball. This will help make it easier to win the point.

### Running through the drop shot

Whatever body weight you have going through the shot will make it easier to get the ball over the net. Slow down as you're making contact with the ball so you have more control with your forward momentum. This will help you have more control attempting the drop shot.

### Approach shot

Grips of choice - Eastern Forehand, Semi-Western, Full Western or Continental for slicing or volley.

An Approach shot : Attempting to hit a ground stroke while moving forward in no man's land (the area between the service box line and the baseline), near the service box line, or in the service box. For that matter anywhere on the court inside the baseline that requires you to move forward to approach the ball in a effort to hit a ground stroke or an approach volley.

### FAQ's

1) **Why do I keep hitting my approach shots into the net.** There are 4 very good reasons why this happens. First and foremost is taking your eye off the ball. Avoid looking over the net at the intended target as you're making contact with the ball. Second, as you make contact with the ball don't come up and across too early without hitting out through the ball first. Hitting out through the ball combined with keeping your head perfectly still as if you're posing for a picture at contact will make hitting approach shots a lot more fun and successful. Third, don't let the ball descend

below the top of the net. Be sure to hit at the apex ( top of the bounce). At that point the ball should be higher than the net so now you can hit aggressively straight through the ball with the horizontal ground stroke with a greater amount of pace and still keep the ball within the lines. Last but not least, be sure you don't end the path of the stroke down below your waist but rather end the racket path of the stroke above your opposite shoulder. This will prevent you from hitting down into the net as easily.

2) **Why do I keep hitting my approach shots out**. Either you're letting the ball descend below the top of the net and/or you're trying to hit the ball too hard when you're having to hit up and over the net. That makes your chances of hitting out greater unless you have a tremendous amount of topspin on the ball. Or you're hitting with an open racket face by hitting under the ball without any topspin.

**Overcoming Natural Tendencies**
**For the Approach Shot**
**Not freezing your head as you watch the ball at contact**

That will cause you lift your head to look over the net too soon at the intended target. Once your head starts to lift to look over the net your racket head will lift from the hitting zone causing you to brush across the ball prematurely instead of hitting through the contact point. Being off balance with your weight on the wrong foot will still give you a better chance of keeping the ball in play when keeping your head perfectly still at contact. I've seen so many club and recreational players as well as pros with the best form and perfect balance miss shots that otherwise they would not have missed, if only for freezing their head as they watched the ball at contact. I have students that don't have perfect technique but are so steady and consistent because of the tremendous concentration of freezing their head as they watch the ball at contact. If you can resist the temptation of looking over the net at your target, you'll be so amazed how consistently fast your level will rise from just controlling your head by staying completely still as you watch the ball at contact. Once you develop this muscle memory you will have wished you started doing this a long time ago.

## Waiting for the ball

Imagine you freezing your head as you watch the ball at contact. Now focus on <u>going to the ball.</u> Don't wait for the ball to come to you or don't let the ball <u>play</u> you. Waiting for the ball on the approach shot (this is a ball that's inside the service box or no man's land) allows the ball to play you. As you approach the ball try to make contact at the top of the bounce (the apex). An approach shot usually is in the pressuring zone (no man's land) or the point ending zone (inside the service box). The pressuring zone is the area on the court that is anywhere from no man's land (that's the area between the baseline and the service box line) to just inside the service box. The point ending zone is just inside the service box area to the net. At this position you'll have a major advantage of hitting an offensive shot because the ball will be higher than the net. This will allow you to hit through the shot with authority, as opposed to letting the ball drop below the top of the net and having to hit up and over the net. Keep in mind the closer you are to the net the larger the percentage of the court becomes available to hit into. Your percentage of hitting a winner is much greater. The further away from the net the court percentage becomes smaller and more difficult to hit an outright winner. A helpful tip is as the ball starts to rise, start moving to the ball to make contact at the top of the bounce. Having the mindset to be ready to move to the ball will help in playing more aggressively. Without that mindset you'll find yourself waiting for the ball to come to you and descend and that will force you to hit more defensively by having to hit up and over the net, giving your opponent time to get in position. Keep in mind this game is about time, place, angles, and options. When you hit the ball at the apex (top of the bounce) you have just taken time away from your opponent to get into place.

Hitting at the apex allows you more options and angles. Remember: freeze your head as you watch the ball at contact.

## Hitting to your opponents' stronger stroke

Hitting to your opponents' stronger stroke is giving them a better chance of returning your approach shot. Usually the forehand is the stronger stroke for most players because it is more natural. Once in a while you come across a player that favors his backhand, but I recommend hitting to the backhand. Most backhands result in returns that come back high and weak, (especially one-handed backhands) or simply cause an unforced error. When confronted with a player that has a good one or two-handed backhand as well as a forehand, you will still stand a better chance by going to their backhand. More of this will be discussed in "Basic Strategy."

## Racket not back

Approaching the ball without having your racket back at 6 o'clock (facing the back fence behind you, on that imaginary clock you're standing in the middle of) will make it more difficult to time the ball at the top of the bounce or earlier. It will force you to rush back with the racket only to find yourself rushing forward to make contact at 9 o'clock (contact point) for a forehand approach shot, rather than making contact out in front of your front foot for more control. It's a natural tendency for most people to get the racket back too slowly then finding themselves rushing forward in a state of panic to hit the ball. In actuality, you should be doing the opposite. If you get the racket back at 6 o'clock (facing the back fence behind you) quickly, you can now swing forward in a slow and smooth controlled motion to make contact at 9 o'clock. With very fast-paced balls you 'll have control with little stress and effort. With constant practice and repetition you will learn to prepare earlier instinctively. Another helpful reminder, when focusing on the ball coming over the net, start preparing your racket back to 6 o'clock (facing the back fence behind you) before the ball bounces in front of you. Once you are in position, all you need to do is concentrate on swinging forward smoothly with more control to make contact at 9 o'clock (contact point). But don't forget racket head acceleration will pick up at 8 o'clock to make contact at 9 o'clock for a cleaner and a more controlled stroke on the forehand groundstroke approach shot. If you swing with full acceleration from 6 o'clock to 9 o'clock you will not hit the sweet spot as easily and will not find your rhythm needed to hit with control. The same goes for a backhand approach shot. In this regard for more control you accelerate the racket from 4 to 3 o'clock.

## Over Head Smash

**Problem**.................. Hitting into net, long or completely missing the ball.

**Natural Tendency**.. Dropping head, not letting the ball bounce first.

**Result**.................... Miss hit, hitting long, hitting into net, ball dropping too low, not going up to the ball.

**Cure**....................... Keep your head up as if looking at the sky. Take your non hitting arm and aim it at the ball to track the ball. Be sure to keep the non hitting arm up long enough to follow the ball at the contact point. **(Photo 7A)** If you drop your arm too soon your head will have the tendency to drop. When you keep your head up you actually can feel the pulling of your neck muscles under your chin. Be to sure to position yourself sideways to the net and behind the ball. Don't let the ball get behind you. Once that happens your weight will be on the wrong foot ( back foot ) which results in hitting long, into the net or any number of errors. Try to make contact in front and above your head at 12 or 11:00 o'clock (for left handed player, 1:00 or 12 o'clock for right handed players) just as you would to serve. Imagine reaching up and over the ball. It's a natural tendency to hit down on the ball when you drop your head. Another important point is to have both arms up above your head at the same time as if to say

"Hurray!" for preparation in hitting the overhead smash. Your left arm (racket arm if you're left-handed) will be up above your head as if talking on a telephone. This will make it easier to time the ball out of the air. If your racket is lagging too far down waist level or below, it's much to difficult to time the ball at contact above your head at 12 or 11:00 o'clock. Whenever the sun is an issue it's usually wise to let the ball bounce first. With this in mind you can prepare yourself to hit at a slightly lower height. If the sun continues to still be a problem, your best alternative is to let the ball drop low enough to hit a ground stroke. The grip of choice is the Continental. (Refer to the chapter, "Grips"). Otherwise the Eastern Forehand will work just as well. You must instinctively know when the ball is dropping too low in an attempt to hit an overhead smash, so you can be prepared to hit a high volley instead. Attempting to hit an overhead smash when the ball drops too low will cause you to hit long or into the net. (Positioned sideways to the net and looking at the ball)

**Photo 7A**

## Overcoming Natural Tendencies
## For the Overhead Smash

### Dropping your head

Dropping your head at contact will cause you to hit into the net, miss hit, hit long, or simply miss the ball all together. To correct this, freeze your head as you watch the ball at contact by concentrating on the color of the ball. You can also look for the blur of the the racket head through the contact.

## Contact point too low

Waiting for the ball is the prime reason the contact is too low. As you prepare to position yourself sideways with your right shoulder facing the net (with the imaginary clock *standing just to the left of you)*, your right arm should be up at 12 o'clock tracking the ball and your racket above your head with your elbow positioned about 9 o'clock. Reach up to the ball as if to" high five" it. Always have the mind set to go up to the ball as you would with the serve. Be sure that contact is made in front and above your head out into the court with your body weight exploding up and out to the ball.

## Not letting the ball bounce

Hitting the ball out of the air is always very difficult (even for the pros) because it travels at unpredictable speeds on every over head smash. The sun can also factor in and make it more difficult. Let the ball bounce first - especially if the lob is extremely high and pushes you back deep to the base line. At this point have the mind set of serving into the whole court instead of the much smaller service box. It would be wise to use a lot of spin for a smaller margin of error. Just as in your service motion don't pause or have a hitch. A continuous motion with a great amount of racket head speed just before you're ready to make contact with the ball will make the stroke a formidable weapon. Strive for accuracy and placement first, then power.

## Racket not in ready position

Having your racket hanging down below your waist makes it difficult to time the ball perfectly at contact in front and above your head at 12 or 11 o'clock. Having both arms up at the same time as if to say "Hurray!" will make it easier to time the ball at contact in an upward and forward striking motion in front and above your head. When the racket is up in the proper position, your right arm (the non-hitting arm) will be positioned at 12 o'clock tracking the ball and your left arm (racket arm) will be positioned just above your head almost as if your talking on a telephone.

## Non- hitting arm not tracking ball

Keeping your non hitting arm up to track the ball long enough will help to keep your head up at contact. The moment your non- hitting arm drops, your head is likely to follow resulting in an error. When watching the ball at the point of contact freeze your head for accuracy and consistency.

## Contact too far behind head

Position yourself side ways to the net and behind the ball during contact. Once the ball gets passed you, you're in a defensive position with your weight on the wrong foot (back foot). At that point the ball has played you instead of you playing the ball. You want to be far enough back so you can take two steps forward into the shot to exchange your weight from your back foot to your front foot for better weight exchange, balance and power.

## Overhead smash not practiced enough

It's natural to walk out on a tennis court and immediately start to work on your ground strokes, then some volleys and a few overheads. But with most recreation and club players you'll see a frequent amount of lobs. So it stands to reason that the overhead smash should be a shot that one would want to do very well. In order to execute it well with confidence you have to spend as much or more time practicing this very difficult shot every time you walk out on the tennis court. The overhead smash is a very important shot because it allows you the opportunity to be aggressive and take control of the point or to hit a winner. But the overhead smash is one of the most difficult shots in the game for most people. The ball is usually falling out of the sky at unpredictable speeds on every overhead, and the sun and wind can often be a factor. When you don't practice the overhead smash enough you'll find yourself getting tight, which results in making an error by hitting into the net, long, or simply missing the ball completely – mostly due to dropping your head at contact. Once your head drops, your racket head drops. Make it a point to practice this shot as much as possible, and you will soon find yourself far more relaxed and looking forward to the next opportunity to hit an overhead smash.

### Dropping your non-hitting arm too soon

Dropping your non hitting arm too soon when tracking the ball out of the sky will cause your head to drop too. Try to keep the non hitting arm up long enough to make solid contact with the ball to help keep your head up longer. Watch the ball at the point of contact and Freeze Your Head!

### Hitting the ball out of the air instead of letting the ball bounce first

Hitting the ball out of the air on the overhead smash is what we see the pros do most of the time. When the sun and wind is a major factor or if you're moving back and you're caught on the wrong foot, let the ball bounce first. Position yourself sideways to the net as you would when you serve and be sure you are far enough behind the ball so it allows you to take two steps forward into the shot with your body weight moving forward. Watch the ball at the point of contact and freeze your head.

### The Lob

**Problem**.................. Not enough height, lack of control.

**Natural Tendency**.. Slapping at the ball, using too much wrist, attempting to use too much spin.

**Result**...................... Lack of control, hitting the ball too long, hitting into the net, or just hitting wide.

**Cure**........................ Bend your knees and keep your racket arm straight without bending at the elbow or the wrist. **(Photo 7B)**. Make contact under the ball in the attempt to hit high and deep over your opponent's head. This would be a defensive lob. A defensive lob is primarily used to buy you some time to get back in position, but it can also be used to hit a winner. To hit an offense of lob you would hit with a lower arc over your opponent's head in the attempt to hit an outright winner. Usually the offensive lob is hit with topspin.

**Photo 7B**

The lob is a stroke I feel doesn't get the credit it deserves. When used properly the lob can be a very effective stroke in guaranteeing a point to win, for example, when your opponent is looking into the sun. Also keep in mind that most players have a difficult time hitting the overhead smash simply because the overhead smash isn't practiced as much as the groundstrokes.

There are two kinds of lobs: an offensive lob and a defensive lob. An offensive lob is used when you are going for a point with the height and arc of the lob just high enough over your opponents head that you can hit with topspin. A defensive lob arcs much higher over your opponent, buying you time to get prepared for the next shot by getting yourself back into position. The lob is used mostly in doubles with club and recreational players that range from the levels 2.5 to 4.5 but it's used in singles as well. One of the main reasons the lob is used so often at this level is because the players are out of position by playing too close to the net and the groundstrokes are not hit with as much pace and penetration. It is a lot easier to hit a lob off of a 40 to 75 mile an hour groundstroke as opposed to a higher level players who hit the ball much harder with groundstrokes averaging 80 or 90 miles an hour.

To hit a defensive lob you should have the racket face open under the ball facing the sky holding either the Continental Grip or the Eastern Forehand. This allows the racket face to be at a convenient angle on the ball. The Semi-Western, Full Western and the Eastern Forehand Grip can also be applied if you are attempting to hit an offensive lob to win the point by imparting a great amount of spin. These three grips allow the angle of the racket face to be on the ball to conveniently hit with a significant amount of spin with the intention of winning the point. A good strategy for hitting a lob is hitting crosscourt and / or to your opponent's backhand. The backhand overhead smash is one of the most difficult shots in the game of tennis. Most backhands are weaker than forehands especially when it comes to the overhead smash, which by itself is a very difficult shot and especially the backhand overhead smash. Do not lose sight that a tennis court is longer on an angle. It stands to reason when you lob on an angle your margin for error will be smaller as opposed to a lob straight up or down the line. Use the lob wisely and it will be a very effective and reliable way of winning a point. However, players usually frown over- using the lob because it's not much fun having to hit moon balls. It is considered by most to be an undesirable way to play the game of tennis.

## Overcoming Natural Tendencies
## For the Lob

### Not freezing head when watching
### the ball at point of contact

Typical problem as with all of the strokes, looking at the intended target as you're making contact with the ball.

### Wrist not firm at contact

Using too much wrist will result in slapping at the ball and cause you to lose control of the shot. For a defensive lob have a firm wrist in a locked position and hit under the ball with the intentions of hitting with a greater amount of height over the net. For the offensive lob have a firm but relaxed wrist as hitting your groundstrokes. You'll have more control for hitting with a lower arc but high enough over your opponents head with topspin by brushing up the back side of the ball as on your groundstrokes.

### Not bending at the knees

When you bend at the waist your not allowing yourself to get down under the ball as easily. Bend at the knees for more control and for better access to getting down to the ball.

### Too much body movement

For more control when attempting a lob think of using your arm only and less body movement by twisting and turning and lifting up.

### Attempting to hit with too much spin

This is a common problem when first learning to hit a lob. Most people will hit with spin by trying to brush up the backside of the ball. Learn first to come under the ball to get a better feel of attempting the easier defensive lob. Once you feel you've develop that muscle memory, attempt the more difficult offensive lob which requires brushing up the backside of the ball with topspin.

### Bending your arm at the elbow and wrist

For a more controlled lob keep your arm straight without bending at the elbow or the wrist. Once you start breaking your arm at the elbow and wrist you lessen your chance of consistency.

# Basic Footwork

Footwork is a part of tennis that comes easy for some players but not for all. Some people are naturally light on their feet. Roger Federer appears to float around the court. That has a lot to do with great anticipation which makes it appear that he knows where his opponent is going to hit the ball. I've noticed in my years of teaching that my students who had the best footwork, as strange as it may sound, were fairly good dancers. Staying relaxed and learning to concentrate on just the ball coming off your opponent's racket helps you develop great anticipation and better balance. The key is being relaxed and limber and learning to try to read your opponent's racquet head.

If you watch the intricacies of footwork of some of the best tennis players in the world such as Roger Federer, Rafael Nadal, Pete Sampras, Andre Agassi and others, you may notice that they live on the balls of their feet when playing a match. Their anticipation is great because they are always ready to split step (landing on the balls of your feet shoulder width apart) with perfect balance just before their opponent is ready to make contact with the ball. You'll also notice that the greats will take large steps to cover a lot of ground to be sure they get to the ball, just so they can apply the brakes by taking smaller steps to prepare themselves for the final stance with perfect balance.

The natural tendency mistake that beginners, club and recreational players make is taking large steps all the way to the point they want to hit the ball. They end up either overrunning the shot or running into the ball. Instead, take large steps (as if sprinting) to get you to the ball as quickly as possible. As you approach the point of contact slow down by taking little steps to balance yourself to hit the shot. You might not notice that every time you watch your favorite tennis star they will split step no matter where they are on the court just before their opponent is ready to make contact with the ball.

This is also the case in the Point Ending Zone (or service box). When the opponent is getting ready to hit the ball they will split step to prepare themselves with perfect balance to hit a volley. As the toss leaves the server's hand the returner moves forward and splits step as the server makes contact with the ball. Split stepping prepares you to explode in either direction. That's not possible if you are back on the heels or flat-footed. Full concentration should be on the ball coming off your opponent's racquet head. Land on the balls of your feet in a split step shoulder width apart as your opponent is making contact with the ball.

# Practicing

Practice, practice, practice. We hear it all the time. Practice is good but only if you're practicing in the correct way and not developing bad habits. So often I've seen dedicated tennis players spending hours practicing with the incorrect techniques and inadvertently developing bad habits which are harder to break in the long run. Spending hours practicing the wrong way is not nearly as productive as practicing for a short period of time in the correct way.

For starters, take a lesson from a qualified USPTA certified instructor. Learn the correct way to perform one or two strokes in a lesson. I often suggest that my students bring a tablet to take notes. Once you have the proper technique for that stroke, it's up to you to practice enough to develop the muscle memory needed for the mechanics of the stroke to become instinctive. Thinking too much will only confuse you and prevent you from executing the stroke properly. I've known people who have played for years with the wrong technique but are very consistent in the game. The only problem is they get to a certain level and that's as good as they're going to get. If you want to be the best player you are capable of being, you need to learn the proper techniques.

The simplest and most economical way to practice is with a ball hopper full of tennis balls. Forget about a ball machine or practicing against the wall for now.

Practicing against a wall is one of the best ways to develop your strokes, timing, and stamina. However, it's only good for players who can control the ball with reasonable technique. Otherwise, you'll spend most of your valuable practice time chasing balls over the wall. When practicing on a wall, keep in mind the distance from the net to the baseline is 39 feet. Measure this distance so you can have a realistic feel of the time needed to prepare your racquet back to 6 o'clock (facing the back fence behind you). Start out swinging slowly so you develop your timing along with warming up cold muscles properly. Most importantly, develop the muscle memory of <u>freezing your head at contact as you watch the ball.</u> Don't look at the wall until you hear the ball hit, and then look up quickly. This will help tremendously in disciplining yourself to control your head from not moving before making contact with the ball.

Looking across the net at the intended target is the #1 natural tendency mistake. Your feet could be out of position or you could be off balance with your weight on the wrong foot, but freezing your head as you watch the ball at contact will give you a much better chance of consistency as well as keeping the ball in play. Practice keeping your head still and you will be amazed how you'll be able to turn a defensive shot into an offensive shot. Having great foot work, balance, preparation, and good technique along with freezing your head as you watch the ball at contact is and should be your ultimate goal. Ball machines are good to work out on, but they take unnecessary time that's needed when just starting to develop muscle memory and proper technique.

## A Simple Concept for Practicing Your Groundstrokes

Situate a ball hopper behind you to the right at an easy reaching distance so you can reach back and grab the next ball with your right hand to help you develop a rhythm for practicing. For developing your strokes, simply toss the ball out in front of you to the right so you can step into the shot having your weight going forward. It is important that you perform the stroke technically correct. I recommend you repeat this motion as much as possible because repetition with the proper technique is the key. Be certain the mechanics and the technique are correct. Once you feel you are becoming more consistent with the proper technique, seek out someone who just wants to hit. If you play for points too soon your natural tendency will force you to go back to your bad habits. It doesn't matter if you get the ball on one or two bounces. When you do get to the ball, <u>freeze your head as you watch the ball at contact</u> with the proper technique and follow through.

Try your best not to be overly concerned about your balance and footwork at this point. Focus on one important part at a time when developing a stroke. Once you get more consistent, bringing in a ball machine is helpful. Place the ball machine in the middle of the court just behind the baseline without topspin and without oscillation. Be sure the balls are landing as close as possible to the same spot just so you can focus on the stroke itself and not worry about your foot work or having to move to the ball. Once you feel confident, take it a step further by moving two or three steps to the left where you have to move to the ball to hit a forehand. Stand in closer to the bounce so you can experience different depths. This will help you develop the timing for hitting the ball on the rise.

Change the machine to shoot the balls with a little topspin, under spin and flat to help you develop your timing. If you continue to hit the ball on the rise or at the apex while <u>freezing your head as you watch the ball at contact,</u> your level will rise and you will be far more dangerous. By learning to hit early you give your opponent less time to get in position. When practicing placement don't look over the net at the intended target. Aim with the palm of your hand in the direction you want to place the ball That's the direction your racquet head will be facing. Looking over the net at the intended target won't help your accuracy nearly as much as learning to direct the ball without looking over the net. When you finally learn to do this, your confidence level will rise dramatically.

Learn to find your rhythm to keep the ball in play. Preparing your racquet back to six o'clock (facing the back fence behind you) early enables you to swing forward slowly and smoothly with control. I believe in having as many "weapons" as your ability allows. To develop weapons is to be capable of hitting with pace, depth and authority on a reliable and consistent basis. In order to achieve this you must have tremendous racquet head speed, proper technique and good timing. This requires many hours of dedicated practice. The more you hit and rally to perfect your strokes, the faster you'll learn by trial and error. That's why I stress the point to rally with anyone available as much as possible when working on perfecting your strokes.

If you're lucky enough to have someone to practice with, a good concept is having your practice partner stand next to you dropping balls for you to repeatedly hit the stroke over and over again. As boring as it might sound, it is a very effective and economical way to develop muscle memory. Have your hitting partner feed rapidly to help in practicing quick recovery after each hit. After several ball hoppers of this drill on both forehand and backhand, have your hitting partner step back closer to the net off to the side in the alley and feed balls to you with a variety of depths. This will familiarize you with hitting the ball on the rise and at the top of the bounce or when the ball is descending. This drill is best when the feeder pitches the ball consistently with the same pace. A rapid feed from the same distance speeds up recovery time for developing faster footwork.

The groundstrokes and the serve are the only strokes you can practice alone without the use of a practice wall or a ball machine. The more you dedicate yourself to practicing, the faster you will develop the muscle memory required to play instinctively. Practicing all other strokes such as volleys, half volleys, high volleys, swing volleys, overhead smash and lobs with a practice partner that has the same goals you have will help you  progress at a faster pace.

Most players have a weakness whether it's a serve without pace or a badly missed timed overhead smash. One of the common problems I see is players with weaker backhands. Backhands - especially one-handed backhands - tend to float back weak and high.  Players will often run around their backhand to hit a forehand. My suggestion when learning to develop weapons on both sides is to resist running around your backhand. Confront your weakness until it no longer exists. With this kind of discipline and dedicated practice you will no longer have a weak side for your opponents to exploit. This goes for all your strokes. Isolate your biggest fear, confront it, analyze it, and break it down. If you have no idea what the problem is, it's time to consult a USPTA certified instructor. Once you understand the correct technique it is up to you to practice the stroke enough to do it instinctively. Don't give up on it. Do it until you know it's perfect. Practice like it means as much to you as if you are playing in a match. I guarantee your results will be self satisfying and rewarding.

A good way to practice groundstrokes along with your doubles game is to rally with four people who stay at the baseline unless forced to come in for a short ball or an approach shot. While practicing your serve and volleys more for placement and penetration, this drill is valuable in helping you be mentally prepared to pounce on any short ball and learn to control the net. I've found this drill helps in finding your range for groundstrokes and learning to be mentally aggressive for the short ball. Play to 11, but you have to win by 2 points. Any one of the four players can start the feed. The only stipulation is you have to serve underhand and from behind the baseline. You can't come in unless a short ball forces you in. After the best out of five games, rotate clockwise to play with a new partner and on a new side. This is the time for the feeder to serve overhand. The only stipulation is you get just one serve and you can't come in until you get a short ball. Anyone can start the feed with only one serve. Once you've come in for a short ball, lobs are not allowed. Your opponent can hit any other shot except the lob, so they are forced to try to pass you. Doing so forces you to have to play more aggressively which raises your level.

### Learning to play in the Wind

When I am asked about the best way to deal with playing in the wind, I advise players to take notice of the obvious. Are you hitting into the wind or is the wind behind you? The best strategy is to hit with less pace and more topspin when the wind is behind you for higher percentage tennis. Even without the wind when you hit a flat ball you have a much better chance of the ball going long. Take notice if the wind is blowing across the tennis court east to west or west to east. In either case don't aim too close to the side lines but toward the middle of the court. Learn to adjust your range by hitting with more pace or less pace depending on whether the wind is at your back or in your face.

Take notice if your opponent is right-handed or left-handed. If he or she is right-handed and you're playing on a windy day, use that to your advantage to hit to their backhand. Backhands on any kind of day are usually weaker and a windy day just compounds the problem for your opponent. Take control of the point by being totally aware of the moment. If you don't take advantage of the moment, you sacrifice a good opportunity to either force an unforced error or hit an outright winner. You will have the advantage (especially on a windy day) when you freeze your head as you watch the ball at contact. Watch the ball into your strings until you finish the stroke first.

I've always found it interesting that many tennis players complain about playing in the wind. Being fully aware which way the wind is blowing helps to adjust to the ball and gives you the immediate advantage of knowing that you'll make solid contact with control far more often than your opponent. Mix up your shots to keep your opponent off balance. Think more in terms of playing by guile rather than brute force and the wind will be your friend.

## Learning to serve into the Sun

Learning to serve into the sun is a major problem for most tennis players, including me. What I find works very well is to keep your head down looking toward the ground as your tossing motion goes up. Just before you release the ball, quickly look up to make contact with the ball. You may be forced to adjust your toss slightly and hit with more spin for higher service percentage. Or, if you have a high toss, bringing it down a little lower will sometimes be the only adjustment needed. If you cannot adjust, wearing a cap, sunglasses or combination of both will most definitely make it easier or even take care of the problem.

## Drills To Improve Your Game

### Pressure Tennis

To improve your serve it's important to practice in a practical way. Everyone would like to serve like their favorite tennis star. Depending on how much effort you put into learning the correct technique from a professional instructor, it takes dedication and a lot of hard work to be able to achieve a formidable serve. Whether your aim is to serve as good as the #1 player in the world or to serve as good as your ability allows, the best way to approach it is to play a little game with yourself called pressure tennis. You get a first and second serve just as you would in a match, but you're playing against yourself. If you miss both serves in either deuce court or ad court, the point goes against you (such as love 30). You can do a complete set this way. Stay focused on consistency and not power. Concentrate on placement. After you feel you can place the serve consistently and win the set, start thinking about power. Keep in mind most tennis players are only as good as their second serve. So it's paramount that you learn to develop a very good and reliable second serve in pressure tennis. Try practicing by allowing yourself to serve only your second serve.

### Mini Tennis

Mini tennis helps you incorporate all of the strokes, footwork, and balance that are required to play the game well. Use it as a warm-up, not to play points. Mini tennis consists of two players hitting the ball back and forth without pace from just behind the "T" of the service boxes. It works best when you intentionally hit back to your opponent. The sole purpose is to keep the ball in play by incorporating whatever stroke is needed to keep the rally going. Mini tennis prepares you mentally to have the mindset to move to the ball. When you play correctly you move to the ball and learn to incorporate the same aggressive mindset instinctively as you would while playing the complete court from the baseline.

Playing mini tennis forces you to apply all the strokes such as the half volley, full volley, swing volley, drop shots, overhead smash and groundstrokes. This warm-up drill is especially helpful if you play doubles the majority of the time. It instills the mindset of not allowing the ball to play you. Along with preparation for footwork and balance, it's a great way to learn how to develop soft hands (the ability to hit softly with control). Freezing your head as you watch the ball at contact also helps develop eye -hand coordination and prepares you to warm-up cold muscles slowly the proper way.

### Set Manageable Goals

Be honest with yourself. Thirty-three is considered too old to compete with the best in the world. Even if you're extremely athletic and in the best physical condition possible, you probably will never qualify for the ATP or WTA tour. Strive to be a solid player in whatever level you achieve. Learn to enjoy the game and keep a positive attitude. Don't let vanity or competitiveness rule your game of tennis.

Be willing to put in the time to get the results. Everyone can take lessons from the greatest player in the world, but it won't help if one doesn't not put in the time to practice and understand the dedication it takes to improve and develop muscle memory. It requires a lot of time and effort to practice repetitious drills and take instruction to get to the next level you're striving for.
Be a smart student. Don't expect to become a world-class player without proper instruction. Look for a certified USPTA instructor

that will guide you on the right path to your realistic goals. With the right teacher, you should see improvement in just a few lessons, not a few years. You'll get what you pay for if you watch, learn, and practice consistently and <u>correctly</u>.

Be true to the basics. Practicing the wrong way for 6 hours with the wrong technique is far worse than putting in fewer hours practicing the proper way with the correct technique. Hit balls with any player available regardless of skill level to develop the proper technique and muscle memory. Control your concentration to boost your confidence.

## Racquet Selection

Very Light - 12 ¼ oz. or less
Light – Between 12 ¼ and 13 ¼ oz.
Medium – Between 13 ¼ and 14 ¼ oz.
Heavy - 14 ¼ oz. or more

Selecting a racquet is a personal decision. I never recommend that anyone choose the kind of racquet their instructor uses regardless of the brand and model. I would recommend finding a racquet that feels comfortable and suitable to your level of playing ability. Stay with that racquet so it eventually feels like an extension of your arm. The

classic mistake most people make is changing racquets too often and not giving themselves the chance to develop the natural feel that's experienced over an extended period of time. Depending on your style and level of play, you can find a racquet that's head light, head heavy, or evenly balanced. Choose the size of the racquet head along with the kind of string and tension that best suits your needs.

**Photo 8A** (Head Heavy Racket)

Racquets that are head heavy make it more difficult for the lower level player to exert more control but easier to generate power. A head heavy racquet is usually best for base liners who like to stay on the base line to play the game with extra power. A racquet with weight on the head is more powerful and absorbs shock – something that's helpful for those suffering from arm problems. If you're playing with a racquet that is too light, it will not absorb the shock as easily and could be the cause of lack of power. Even though it is easier for some players to generate more racquet head speed with a headlight racquet, it doesn't translate into power. Power comes from racquet head speed combined with excellent timing and the proper technique. Evenly balanced racquets are a good way to go for some players because they provide some head

**Photo 8B** (Evenly Balanced)

**Photo 8C** (Head Light)

weight for power but are easy to maneuver around the net and easy to modify if you choose to make the racket heavier by applying lead tape.

Another important point to keep in mind is the size of the racquet head. A larger head gives you a larger sweet spot, but makes you less agile to move around the net efficiently for volleys. For some players with slightly impaired vision the larger racquet head size can be an important issue. Regardless of what racket you choose always

FREEZE YOUR HEAD when watching the ball at contact. With the higher level players, it is becoming more popular to use a thin beam with a smaller racquet head simply because it is easy to maneuver around the net and generate the racket head speed required for tremendous power and control.

Don't overlook the importance of the string and tension you choose. A racquet that is strung too tightly will not have the same power as one that is strung loosely. For example, when you string a racket at 60 lbs. you have more control but less power. If you string a racket at 50 lbs. you have more power but less control. According to the string experts, the ball stays on the strings longer at 50 lbs. resulting in more depth that gives the impression of more power. At 60 lbs. the ball leaves the strings much quicker giving more control but lacking depth, penetration, and power. The tighter tension allows you to take a bigger cut at the ball with less chance of hitting long.

# Scoring

| Server wins four points | Receiver wins four points |
|---|---|
| 15 - 0 (fifteen – love) | 0 - 15 (love-fifteen) |
| 30 - 0 (thirty-love) | 0 - 30 (love -thirty) |
| 40 - 0 (forty – love) | 0 - 40 (love-forty) |
| Game to server - (love game) | Game to receiver-(love game) |

Both players win points
1 point each- 15 - 15 (fifteen- all)
2 points each-30 - 30 (thirty-all)
3 points each-40 - 40 (deuce)

Server or Receiver must win two consecutive points; alternate scoring reverts the score to deuce.

## Tiebreaker

The first point is played from the right court with the service alternating. Players change after every six points and at the end of the tiebreaker.

The player serving serves for the first point. The opponent serves for the next 2 points. Each player serves alternately for 2 points until the tiebreaker is decided.

The tiebreaker counts as 1 game for the ball change, but if this change is due at the beginning of the tiebreaker, it is delayed until the 2nd game of the following set.

The player (or pair) who served first in the tiebreaker receive service in the first game of the following set.

The first player (or pair) to win 7 points wins the tiebreaker and a set if he leads by a margin of 2 points (7-0 up to 7-5). If the score is 6 - 6 the tiebreaker continues until one of the players wins by 2 points.

## USTA COMAN TIEBREAK PROCEDURES
## FOR DOUBLES

The Coman Tiebreak Procedure is employed when a game is tied at 6-6 and a seven (7) point tie breaker is played to determine the winner of the game. The first team to win 7 points (by a 2 point margin) wins the game.

In the event that each team has won a game and the set score is 1-1, a ten (10) point Coman tiebreaker is played to determine the winner of the match. The first team to win ten 10 points (by a 2 point margin) wins the match.

### 6-6 Game Score 7 Point Tiebreak

At the end of a 6-6 game:

Next in turn server serves a single point from the DEUCE court.

Teams change respective ends of the court.

Next in-turn server serves two points starting in the AD court. The second point is served from the DEUCE court.

The next in-turn server serves two points starting in the AD court. The second serve is from the DEUCE court.

The teams change ends of the court after every four points (i.e. after the 5th, 9th, 13th points, etc.) until the end of the tiebreak.

First team to win 7 points (by 2 point margin) wins the game.

## Games at 1-1 Set Score 10 Point Tiebreak

At the end of the second set with the score tied at a 1-1 score: this tiebreak is played in lieu of a third game to determine the winner of the match.
Next in turn server serves a single point from the DEUCE court.

Team change respective ends of the court.

Next in-turn server serves two points starting in the AD court. The second serve is from the DEUCE court.

The next in-turn server serves two points starting in the AD court. The second serve is from the DEUCE court.

Teams change end of the court after every four points (i.e .after the 5th, 9th, 13th points, etc.) until the end of the tiebreak.

The first team to win 10 points (by 2 point margin) wins the match.

# Basic Strategy

When we talk about strategy, the same mistakes are made at all levels. Learning to play smarter tactical choices in placing the ball will improve your game before we even talk about power. In recreational play, a high percentage of matches are lost by players making unforced errors as opposed to their opponents hitting outright winners.

All world-class tennis players are basically the same from the neck down. The winning difference is that the great champions are extremely mentally strong and play high percentage tennis. The more you play, the more you'll come across a variety of styles, sizes, and personalities. All those variables should have you take into account how to play your opponent.

I am strong believer in keeping the strategy simple, which helps you play more by instinct. Thinking too much on the court can paralyze you. And of course, freeze your head as you watch the ball at contact.

Tennis is a game of Time, Place, Angles, and Options. Cross court shots have a higher percentage of success than hitting up or down the line.

The dimensions of a tennis court are 78 feet long (23.7 M) by 85.9 feet (26.1 m) corner to corner for doubles. The singles court dimension is 78 feet long baseline to baseline (23.7 M) by 82.5 (25.1m) feet corner to corner. The net is 3 feet high (1m) in the middle and 3.6 feet high (1.1 m) at the sides. In doubles you and your partner are each responsible for covering 18 feet (5.5 m). In singles you are responsible for 27 feet (8.3 M). So it stands to reason hitting crosscourt gives you a larger margin for error. In other words, there is less chance of you making an error by hitting crosscourt. It doesn't matter if you're playing singles or doubles. If you are serious about your tennis you should be practicing with single sticks every time you walk out on the court to practice. This is by far the most violated rule in tennis when playing singles on a doubles court. Using my "Quik -Stiks" every time you practice will create an advantage for you over your opponent. Otherwise, when confronted with single sticks in a tournament they could easily become a physical and psychological distraction.

## The Rule is Perfectly Clear

"When a combined doubles and single court with a doubles net that is used for singles, the net must be supported to the height of 3'6" by means of two post, called "single sticks" which shall not be more than 3 inches square, or 3 inches in diameter. The centre of the single sticks shall be 3 feet outside the singles court on each side."

## Warm-ups

Part of strategy is the simple task of taking notice of your opponent's weaknesses and strengths during the warm-up. Take notice and concentrate on whether certain strokes look unnatural or unorthodox. Believe it or not, some players don't realize they're playing a lefty until the middle of their first set.

Is your opponent short or tall? Does he or she play a one-handed backhand? Do they slice their one-handed backhand most of the time or do they come over it? (If so, that makes them vulnerable to having to play defensively on high bouncing balls, having to hit high bouncing balls with authority on your one-handed backhand is very difficult to nearly impossible). Unless you learn to hit the one-handed backhand early on the rise, you're forced to chip the ball back just to keep it in play. Because it's too high out of your hitting zone above your shoulder, this in turn is giving your opponent a chance to take control of the point. But chipping or slicing the ball back to your opponent who is very tall and is playing a two-handed backhand can be a returner's advantage. With the two-handed backhand you lose the reach you have with a one-handed backhand. That, combined with being tall, makes it more difficult for a better center of gravity and balance. It's a little more taxing for tall players than shorter players to bend down low consistently especially when playing a two-handed backhand. It can be to your advantage if you recognize he or she plays a two-handed backhand but is short or plays a two-handed backhand and is very tall. When your opponent plays a two-handed backhand they should be hitting over the ball 99% of the time. If you notice they are not, that's a sure sign of weakness on that side.

One-handed backhand players can usually play with more variety but the most talented and best players in the world come over the ball the majority of the time. However it is far more difficult with the one-handed backhand. When you have an opponent that plays a one handed backhand and is short, that is an advantage for you.

There are advantages to playing a two-handed backhand for some and a disadvantage for others. It's an advantage for short two-handed backhand player hitting high bouncing balls shoulder height or above on their backhand compared to the one-handed backhand players. With a two-handed backhand your right hand is the dominant hand, so it's like having two forehands. Does your opponent attack the ball early on the rise or do they hit the ball at the apex? Do they choose to wait for the ball to come to them and drop below the top of the net? Hit early and you take time away from your opponent to get in place. Hit at the apex and you have more options available for you to hit the better angles because you're usually making contact above the net which opens the door for more options.

## Basic Strategy for the Game of Singles

Having a bad game plan is better than having no game plan at all. The natural tendency is for players to make the mistake of playing everyone the same way. This is a classic mistake at all levels. When you carefully observe the matches of the great champions, you'll notice that who they are playing determines how they approach that particular match. Everyone has their strengths and weaknesses. Play to their weaknesses and stay focused on what you do best. But, be careful not to play to their weaknesses so much as to give them practice at it.

Observe two players at the 5.5 level battle it out. On a good day they show signs of having the ability to play at the open level - the highest level for non-professional and professionals alike. Let's take the case of two excellent players, one mentally tough but not especially physical and the other physically strong with better strokes, mobility, and speed. Why would the physically stronger and faster player ever lose? He'll lose simply because he's playing short points and going for winners too soon. He is playing low percentage tennis. Instead, he needs to keep the ball in play and move his opponent side to side. By playing longer points he will wear down the mentally tough but physically weaker and slower opponent. On the flip side, being mentally tough has a lot to say for itself. Keeping the ball in play and letting your opponent run himself ragged is also a good game strategy.

Another simple example of strategy is a younger, stronger and faster player who has outstanding strokes being pushed to the limit by a less mobile player twice his age with very average strokes. If the younger player makes the mistakes of trying to win by brute force going for too much and playing short points, it would only take about 10 to 15 minutes to even the odds. By forcing him to play very long points, moving him side to side and bringing him in and pushing him back to the baseline, the younger player starts to show signs of slowing down. Once the legs go, so does the concentration.

It's a simple game strategy but you'd be surprised how often I see this play out on the tennis court. You'd also be surprised how much easier you'll find it if you play more by craftiness than brute force.

As a USPTA certified instructor there's not a style, personality or situation I haven't experienced. For this reason I recommend that all my students hit with anyone regardless of their level of play. Take your ego and put it off to the side and hit with a beginner or someone you know you can hit through. Then hit with someone you know can blow you off the court. The contrast of the level along with the difference in style will only make you a better player. You will see the same kind of ball at times from the highest level player that you would see from a lower level player. You want to put yourself in the position where nothing you are confronted with will surprise you.

A very smart strategy when playing singles is dominating the middle of the tennis court. You want to hit from the middle of the court - from the baseline if possible - even though your angles are not as great. Place your shots to your opponent's corners so he or she is covering more ground than you. Another good tactic to learn is to play half-court tennis. Learn the ability to hit up or down the line with confidence and accuracy at any given opportunity, just as you would when hitting crosscourt groundstrokes. Having this ability promotes the element of surprise by not being predictable. But remember, changing direction is best when you get a short ball. A ball that comes deep with pace crosscourt is wise to hit back in the direction it came from. Pay special attention during the warm-ups if your opponent runs around his backhand to hit more forehands. Are his volleys crisp? Can he volley? Take notice of the technique. If he has poor volley technique during the match a simple and good concept is to bring him in to the net, especially if he is short. It makes for an easy passing shot and/or an easy lob. Usually these players prefer to stay back and pound away from the baseline. We refer to these players as counter punchers. How well does your opponent move during the warm-ups? This is fairly easy to pick up on as long as you make yourself conscious of it. Notice if they have a kick serve during the warm-ups and/ or if they just have a flat or slice serve. The best players will recognize the bounce and be ready to take advantage of that short ball so you can take the opportunity of making contact at the top of the bounce. This will create pressure for your opponent or for you to hit an outright winner. Taking the ball at the top of the bounce allows you the distinct advantage of taking control of the point by hitting through the ball horizontally in a straight line to drive it aggressively. Furthermore, you now have more Angles and Options because of the ball being higher than the net. And let's not forget about Time. You just hit the ball early enough to take Time away from your opponent to get into Place.

## The Three Zones

## Utilize the Zones of the Tennis Court

Rally Zone - The area behind the baseline and about 2 feet into the court. Keep the ball in play by resisting the temptation to go for a winner. Exercise patience. Tennis is a game of Times, Place, Angles, and Options. Hit crosscourt until you get an opportunity to change direction and hit up or down the line. Keep the same racquet head speed to lock into a good rhythm to stay in the rally with some variety. When the opportunity for a short ball arises, take control of the point by changing direction or applying pressure and/or hit an outright winner to an open court.

Pressuring Zone – The no man's land between the baseline and service box. In this zone you have 3 options: 1. Apply pressure and follow in behind your shot. 2. Hit an outright winner. 3. Retreat back to the Rally Zone, because you know instinctively you will not be in proper position at net to win the point. Think of the Pressuring Zone as an opportunity to take control of the point or to hit a winner. Go to the ball to make contact at the top of the bounce.

Point Ending Zone - The service box. At this point you should be in the correct position at the net to end the point. If you don't execute your volley with authority, you will be out of position and your opponent can easily lob or pass you. If you instinctively know you can't win the point on your first volley, the next best option is to volley back to your opponent for better positioning to take control of the point for a winner on the next volley you hit.

### Basic Strategy for Doubles

Singles and doubles are two completely different games. The geometry in playing doubles is far different in many ways. My aim again is to keep the concept of explaining the strategy as simple as possible, especially when describing the game of doubles for those at the level of 3.0 to 4.5 of any age. As with all the strokes in the game, the strategy part of playing doubles has its own natural tendencies that make playing the game of doubles more difficult than needed. I specifically point out this level of play because most public park, club, and recreational players fall into this category. When talking about players at the level of 5.0 to the open level, the game of strategy takes a whole different meaning. Let's first start with the most common natural tendency mistakes and their cures.

# Overcoming Natural Tendencies in
# Strategy for Doubles

1) Server staying back - Staying back will give your opponent many options such as a drop shot, better angles, taking control of the net or hitting outright winners to an open court.

2) Stopping inside the baseline after serving - This will result in hitting your returns from your shoelaces, hitting half volleys, or hitting the ball on the rise which is far more difficult. Not coming in to take control of the net allows your opponent to take control of the point. Stopping inside the baseline to play the point will sometimes encourage you to run back behind the baseline to try and catch up with the ball. This will likely have you hitting it off the wrong foot instead of moving into the volley. Anyway you look at it, playing the game from this position is a disadvantage. Think of the net as a magnet that draws you in to it.

3) Playing too close to the net - This clearly is out of position for 3.0 to 4.0 level. This is one of the biggest mistakes players at this level make. I would not recommend this position unless you are a very high level player. The higher level players can get away with being very close to the net because they hit groundstrokes with greater pace than the lower level players. When you hit groundstrokes like the pros at 80 to 100 mph, it is unlikely you'll be able to hit a lob with control off that kind of pace. Groundstrokes by 3.0 to 4.0 level players are simply are not moving that fast with great penetration. It is much easier to hit a lob off of groundstrokes that are traveling 50 to 80 mph or less.

4) Hitting deep when pulled in for a short ball - The result is you will be out of position by being too close to the net, allowing your opponent to hit a lob. Playing in the middle of the service box is the correct position when playing doubles with your partner serving or returning serve. If you are playing at the 5.0 or open level, you can and probably should be very close to the net at

certain times since the exchange of groundstrokes is far more powerful and penetrating with less chance of your opponent lobbing off an 80 to 100 mile-per-hour groundstroke. With players in the 3.0 level to 4.5 levels the groundstrokes are moving much slower, making is easier to lob off the groundstroke. When you find yourself too far inside the service box at lower-level tennis you are putting yourself out of position with less options. From here you might hit an overhead, volley, a half volley, or even a high volley. Your percentage to hitting to open court is greater but a lob is more likely to happen to <u>you</u>, than you hitting an outright winner in the way of the volley. Playing back just in front the service box line or just behind the service box line is better. From there you will put a stop to the lob and the drop shot. At this level of tennis the lob is used quite a bit and rightfully so. I've heard it said that in this position you're going to end up hitting volleys at your shoelaces. I beg to differ. By being ready to move to the ball, you not only will get the volley earlier but have your weight going forward in the direction of the intended target and not be too close to the net. Remember, in this position it is always easier to move forward as opposed to running back to catch up to a ball that's been hit over your head. You're almost guaranteed not to be in position fast enough to get to the ball quickly enough to be able to transfer your weight forward when making contact with the ball. Not only will your weight be on the wrong foot, but you'll be vulnerable for a drop shot. And smart players will pick up on that immediately. From this modified position at the service line your options in shots are much greater. Only if you move to the ball will you have a greater advantage of hitting your volleys at a higher level above your waist and approach shots at the top of the bounce for better angles, options, and placement to win the point.

5) Serving without variety and placement - The result is being predictable. To serve without being able to purposely place the

ball doesn't help your partner or you. The game of doubles is about playing as a team. It's about assisting your partner and yourself for better positioning on the next ball to win the point. Players who play singles the majority of the time make the mistake of playing the game of doubles the way they play singles. When serving, don't be overly concerned with pace, only placement. The A B Cs of the service box play a major role in placement. They are: Alley, Body, and Center. Learning to consistently place the serve in any one of these positions at any given time is a valuable strategy. As for variety, now we're talking about different spins and heights over the net. For lower-level players, hitting a kick serve is usually not obtainable. The kick serve requires a technique that is difficult to achieve for most players at the level of 3.0 to 4.5. More important is learning to be capable of hitting a slice serve for more variety and, most importantly, helping you to achieve a better and reliable second serve with pace. For most hitting a flat serve with adequate pace is not too difficult. Hitting a flat serve with pace consistently with accuracy is a whole different story. But when you're playing at the 5.0 to open level, you <u>must</u> be able to effectively hit all the serves with pace and accuracy, which would be a flat, slice, and the kick. For those not at that level, a simple part of strategy is to be capable of hitting a flat and slice serve with emphasis on placement and not miles per hour. If you can't hit a flat serve consistently, rely on a very good slice serve for your first serve.

6) Playing doubles like singles -This could be the most common problem with players who normally play singles. They have the tendency to play the game of doubles from the backcourt rather than coming in and cutting off the angles by controlling the net. Wanting to play more by brute force from the backcourt instead of coming in and cutting off the angles by controlling the net is <u>not</u> the best way to approach the game of doubles.

7) Making errors on <u>Second Ball Hit -</u> Almost everyone seems more

concerned about the pace of their serve rather than the placement. Being able to place the serve to help you and your partner anticipate the return is far more important when playing doubles. What frequently happens when you are overly concerned about having more mph is if the return is hit directly back to the server, the second ball that the server hits can result in an error. This also appears to be a problem when having to hit a second ball after your return of serve. Returning the serve well is obviously crucial, but it's the second ball where I often see unforced errors occur that the returner is forced to hit. Much of the time this happens because of being out of position by not being ready to come in to control the net because of stopping in front of the baseline in no man's land. This will often put you in poor position for a difficult shot off your shoelaces or to hit an unanticipated half volley. Playing this modified position just behind the service box line will help tremendously in cutting down any unforced errors because you will be in a better position to have access to all the volleys, low, high, half, and swing volleys and possibly a ground stroke as well as an overhead smash. By coming into your modified position behind the service box line you will likely have access to volleys at waist level if you keep moving to the ball. For those opponents who like to lob and /or drop shot, you've taken their favorite shots out of their repertoire. They now have to figure out another way to get around you which prevents them from playing instinctively. It's much easier to move forward than to have to run back to chase down the ball.

# Tennis Terms

**Ace** - A serve that is untouched.

**All** – The score is even, as in "15 All."

**Apex** -The highest point of the bounce before the ball descends.

**Ball Hog** – A doubles partner who plays balls that are in your territory.

**Baseline** - The line dividing the "out" area from the "in" area made up of the back line of the back court and the small back side of the alleys.

**Bevels** – The eight sides on a racket handle.

**Carry** (also known as a Double Hit)– A legal ball that hits the racket face twice as if to carry the ball across the net.

**Center mark** - The 12" mark at the half way point of the baseline used to distinguish two halves (and service boxes) of a tennis court, or the short mark that bisects the baseline.

**Chop** – A hit under the ball that creates back spin.

**Closed Racket Face** – The hitting surface of the racket is positioned over the ball and facing the ground.

**Contact Zone** - The space between the racquet and the ball just before they make contact.

**Drive** – A ball that is hit hard along a straight line.

**Drop Shot** – A ball that is hit softly with solid under spin.

**Face** – The hitting surface of the racket.

**Fast Court** – Hard cement, wooden, or grass surface.

**Flat** – A hit through the ball hard without spin along a straight line.

**Flatten** – To hit through the center of the ball with a racket that is perpendicular to the ground to generate more pace.

**Foot Fault** – A penalty incurred when the server takes more than one step before making contact with the ball; when the server's foot touches the base line or the back court before making contact with the ball; or when the server's foot extends beyond the imaginary extension of the center mark.

**Hacker** – A player with poor technique.

**Hitting Out** – Fully extending through the ball in the contact zone before finishing the stroke up and across the body.

**Keeping Them Honest** – Intentionally letting the opponent know what shots they can expect you to hit.

**Kick Serve** (also known as a Kicker) – A serve that bounces high and off to the left or right.

**Let** – A serve that hits the top of the net and lands inside the service box; or interference on the court that causes a point to be replayed.

**Miss Hit** – A ball that is unintentionally struck anywhere on the racket other than the center of the strings.

**Mix up** – To use a variety of shots so as not to be predictable.

**Moon balls** - Balls hit from underneath, giving the shot too much height.

**Muscle memory** - Training your brain to repeat an action until it becomes automatic.

**Open Racket Face** – The hitting surface of the racket is positioned under the ball and facing the sky.

**Poaching** – Moving in and across to intercept an incoming ball from the opponent.

**Pressuring zone** – The space between the baseline and the service box.

**Pronate** – To rotate the palm of the hand and the forearm away from the body while making contact with the ball.


**Rally** – A sequence of shots within a point.

**Rally Zone** – The space within the baseline and beyond.

**Return** – The return of a serve to the opponent's court.

**Seed** – A preliminary ranking of players in brackets so that the best players don't meet until later in the competition.

**Service box (**also known as the Point Ending Zone)– The space between the service line and the net that the server must land the ball within.

**Side Spin** – A hit that rotates the ball horizontally (sideways).

**Single Sticks** – Stakes 3' 6" high placed 3 feet outside the singles court in the alley under the net to allow singles play on a doubles court.

**Slice** (also known as Under Spin) – A hit under the ball that causes the ball to rotate toward the player who hit it and away from the opponent.

**Slow court** – Clay surface.

**Supinate** – To rotate the hand or foot toward the body so that the palm or sole is facing upward.

**Sweet Spot** – The center of the racket strings.

**Throat** – The part of the racket between the head and the handle.

**Top Spin** – A hit that rotates the ball toward your opponent.

**Unseeded** – A player not placed in a favored spot in a tournament draw.

**Volley** – To hit the ball before it touches the ground.

**Wheel House** – The hitting zone or striking zone.

# About the Author
# Biography of Frank Sberno

Tennis, always a popular and fun way to relax and stay fit, has been rapidly gaining increasing popularity throughout the nation. The most important item for any player to acquire is a highly competent instructor whose personality, training, enthusiasm, and sheer love of the game is contagious to his students, both novice and seasoned. In this regard, the visitors to and residents of Coachella Valley in Southern California are fortunate to have a primary tennis teacher of the caliber of Frank Sberno.

Frank is a USPTA certified primary tennis instructor who lives and teaches in the Coachella Valley of sunny Southern California. A native of Chicago who visited this area in 1995, he fell in love with it and has never left. He has built a thriving independent practice by being an expert in anything related to tennis and always looking to share his insights into the techniques of the game. Frank is also the inventor on tennis net single sticks called "Quik Stiks" that are sold at Tennis Warehouse, Fromuth, and other sporting goods stores. He teaches at six resorts in the Palm Springs area as well as private homes. Also celebrities have utilized his services and Frank has coached several teams as well.

Peruse this book for valuable tips usually known only to Tennis pros. You will find it entertaining and informative and help you to achieve greater efficiency in the game.

CPSIA information can be obtained
at www.ICGtesting.com
Printed in the USA
FSOW03n1207070116
15381FS

9 780996 533614